Amazon Reader Praise for

The Adversity Advantage

Turn Your Childhood Hardship into Career and Life Success
(Prequel to *Headspace Habits*)

"This book is amazing and has astounding insights that can lead to next level self-awareness and growth. Highly recommend!"

"Loved the book. Very well written. Jude has a way with words and obviously very knowledgeable on the subject of adversity."

"Really helpful way of reframing the effects of adverse childhood experiences. The book shows that personal achievement and satisfaction is achievable despite adverse childhood experiences if the individual is willing to harness their experiences and energies for positive growth."

"Honestly, I must start by saying that I am very resistant to self-help and motivational type books, but this book transcends those genres by far. The depth of research that went into this book is probably what sets it apart and allows it to offer truly meaningful insight—insight that can actually be applied in the real world. It has changed my thinking on a daily basis and has given me new ways to apply my life experiences to my world. It's so worth the read!"

Headspace Habits

Minneapolis

FIRST EDITION JUNE 2024

Headspace Habits: Advice from Zoomers to Boomers

10 9 8 7 6 5 4 3 2 1

Cover design: St. Claire Design Studio

Book design: Gary Lindberg

ISBN: 978-1-962834-13-1

Headspace Habits

ADVICE From Zoomers to Boomers

JUDE MILLER BURKE, PH.D.

Minneapolis

This book is dedicated to all individuals on a journey to understand how traumatic events impacted their lives and who desire to improve the world inside their heads and hearts by learning new habits.

Contents

Also by Jude Miller Burke, Ph.D.

The Millionaire Mystique: How Working Women Become Wealthy – and How You Can Too!

The Adversity Advantage: Turn Your Childhood Hardship into Career and Life Success

Headspace Habits

ADVICE FROM ZOOMERS TO BOOMERS

New Research

JUDE MILLER BURKE, Ph.D.

Minneapolis

Introduction

How do you as an adult face hardship and move forward in life? Most of us have experienced many challenges that require focus and the development of new skills. However, many people do not have the resources or time to go to therapy to learn these skills.

This book clearly outlines researched and practical steps you can take for your self-knowledge and growth to achieve more peace in every aspect of your life. There are multiple assessments for you to evaluate the impact adversity has had on your mind, body, and heart. I have included touching real life interviews and stories to illustrate these points. The *Journey Chart* in the appendix of this book fully explains your pathway to recovery.

This book is a an updated version of my previous book: *The Adversity Advantage: Turn Your Childhood Hardship into Career and Life Success* which was published in 2017 and can be ordered from Amazon. *The Adversity Advantage* was focused on understanding the impact of and overcoming childhood adversity. If you have read *The Adversity Advantage* you will recognize some of the real-life stories, however, the knowledge about overcoming and integrating adverse events, whether as a child or an adult has evolved and has been updated in this book. *Headspace Habits: Advice from Zoomers to Boomers* not only has new information about the impact and recovery from adult and childhood adversity, but new research and stories with recommendations and "cautions" from Generation Z and millennials.

Our daily habits affect our life force—our bodies, emotions, and overall headspace—how you experience and feel about life day in and day out. This topic has even more relevancy today as we have experienced a pandemic and worldwide instability. Our only option is to strengthen ourselves and our families through tried-and-true strategies, recommended by psychologists and people of all ages who have weathered adversity. This requires daily self-care. The research in this book of over four hundred individuals from twenty-two to eighty-two years of age demonstrates the way to calm your headspace resulting in a better relationship with yourself, family, friends, and co-workers. Inspire yourself and learn what to do to enhance the well-being of your mind.

Chapter 1
How *Headspace Habits* Can Help

Is it time to become stronger, more tenacious, and resolute in the face of large and sometimes daily challenges? Hardships become lodged in our bodies and minds, making it more difficult to find peace. How do you calm your headspace enough to turn hardships into life and career success?

It is difficult to admit how our strengths, values, and limitations are determined by who and where we came from. However, we all need to reshape attitudes and behaviors after childhood to achieve personal happiness. That is the genesis of this book: I want to show readers what habits and attitudes help turn their hardships into life satisfaction and happiness, thereby helping them thrive as an adult during times of crisis at home and at work. This book is revised with new research and updated information about the impact and recovery from adversity.

In 2022 I worked with two psychology graduate students, Shannon Burke and Steven Rodriguez, to design and implement a research survey examining the negative impacts of the pandemic on young adults and what behaviors and attitudes helped them thrive. Generation Z (zoomers) and millennials had sage insight into how their lives were impacted personally and professionally, their unhealthy choices, and recommendations to thrive. They were articulate in describing the negative impact and unexpected positives of living through a pandemic.

This recent research, blended with my previous studies about how boomers overcame adversity to achieve personal and professional success, is woven throughout the chapters in this book. The result is knowledge and recommendations from four hundred individuals ages twenty-two to eighty-two on how to weather childhood and adult hardships.

The questions I will help you answer with the real-life stories, research knowledge, and assessments in this book are:

- How has the adversity you experienced as a child formed your worldview and impacted your relationships with family and friends?

- What are your specific inherent and learned strengths and limitations when facing crises, such as the Covid-19 pandemic?

- What do zoomers, millenials, boomers, and social science researchers recommend to cope well with a pandemic or other widespread crises? How are the recommendations similar or different from what long standing research recommends?

The suggestions in this book are informed by my thirty years of experience providing therapy and coaching to clients and research of four hundred people about how they transformed their adversity into helpful survival skills.

While doing research for my previous book, *The Millionaire Mystique: How Working Women Become Wealthy & You Can Too!*,[1] I was struck by one fact that could not be ignored. People who experienced serious troubles in childhood, were as likely to have successful personal and professional lives as anyone else in my study group. Since childhood problems did not limit success, I wondered if the adversity might make some people stronger, allowing them to better weather life detours and failures. Could adversity, in general, actually build hard-earned strengths and survival skills?

The truly surprising thing to emerge from my research is how many people successfully overcome their childhood struggles and go on to lead admirable, productive lives. In fact, more than 60 percent of my sample of people earning at least upper-middle-class incomes reported some kind of misfortune in their early lives. This suffering included poverty, deaths in the family, divorce, physical and verbal abuse, alcoholism, and the witnessing of domestic violence.

I became intensely curious about how people in these circumstances could achieve so much when they had started with so little. Talking to them and studying their lives gave me insights into their motivations, personalities, and the techniques and beliefs that helped them overcome their challenging childhoods. *Headspace Habits: ADVICE From Zoomers to Boomers* tells compelling and real stories of people's lives; however, I have changed their names out of respect for the hardships they survived.

This book will not only be helpful for those who experienced childhood adversity, but for those individuals who have weathered adversity as an adult. One goal of this book is to make more understandable the personal and work lives of people who grew up in families with severe misfortune, and thus help them thrive.

The other goal is to help people who have undergone childhood adversity learn how to turn hard-won childhood survival skills into success and happiness. It is time to stop saying, "It didn't bother me. I am over it." How many times are these denials followed by depression, anxiety, excessive drinking or inappropriate anger?

If this is you, it is time to reach your full potential by using your adversity advantages.

Surprise: Childhood Hardship Is Not a Self-Fulfilling Prophecy

Dr. Mark Attridge, a Minneapolis-based social science researcher, and I have done extensive research on factors that lead to personal and work success. Our work clearly demonstrated that childhood adversity is very impactful and also common. We completed research on a group of high-achieving men and women. On average, participants earned $250,000 annually and had overcome adversity to create happy personal lives. This research project was aimed at identifying the factors that made these men and women successful, including their personality traits, family backgrounds, work styles, work engagement, social influence, foundational work experiences, leadership styles, and communication styles.

One of the unexpected findings was the amount and variability of the childhood problems *both sexes* had prior to becoming successful. Forty percent were abused as children, witnessed domestic violence, or had an alcoholic parent.

The study results led us to gather more data and interviews to focus specifically on the strategies these successful people employed to overcome childhood adversity and develop the resilience and tenacity to create strong families and work success.

In the final phase of our *Adversity and Success* research, we asked 310 men and women to describe how they had resolved the lingering psychological fallout of their early lives. We probed into how they had come to understand and accept their past, cope under duress, and use the hard-won skills to manage challenges as an adult.

Among the helpful things they told us:

- "I know now how wrong these events were for a parent. Somehow I had the knowledge that one day I would be strong enough to stop the abuse and would never pass the abuse on to another generation."

- "I realized that my life was controlled by others. What I thought of as 'normal' was in reality just one way of being. As an adult, you get to create your own life. Don't focus on what you should have had in the past. Instead, focus on what you want your life to be like. Create a vision, share it with others, and work to make your vision a reality."

Even more significantly, we discovered that the number of successful men and women who had experienced ongoing childhood physical and emotional abuse, witnessed domestic violence in their homes, or had an alcoholic or substance-abusing family member (most often a parent) either matched or exceeded the percentage in the general population.[2] In other words, the family backgrounds of these successful and happy individuals were not particularly different from the general population or average earner. Somehow, though, they had been able to transform themselves into engines of success despite the adversity of their early years.

Working Through It

In this book you will learn how a chaotic childhood can be transformed into life satisfaction if you understand and work to integrate the experience. You will learn how to:

- Identify the lingering behaviors and attitudes that harm your relationships with yourself, family, and friends.

- Identify and develop your strengths and healthy coping strategies to calm your mind.

- Learn to regulate your emotions.

- Tap into your psychological strength to bolster self-esteem and a sense of control over your life.

- Respond positively to behavior in others at home and work in spite of emotional triggers from childhood memories.

- Build positive relationships necessary for life success.

The real value of this book is that it will provide specific steps to a recovery pathway and self-assessments to learn how to remedy problems at home or with co-workers, ensuring you function as your best self. The goal is to name, tame, and teach yourself how to overcome past sorrows and choose wiser and healthier behaviors to feel better about yourself and others.

Here's a summary of what you will learn in each chapter.

"Identify Your Emotional Triggers" presents the story of a young professional, Emma, confronting inappropriately expressed anger at work. You may recognize yourself, friends, or family members. This chapter provides a self-assessment to help you understand the situations that flood you with overwhelming emotions or counterproductive behavior. You will learn which of your behaviors to enhance and which to minimize as you attempt to preserve a professional demeanor and emotional intelligence.

"Uproot Family Dysfunction" includes The Adverse Childhood Experiences (ACE) checklist to help you identify the level of trauma you experienced as a child and then provides a roadmap to strengthen your resiliency to help you move beyond your childhood.

The chapter delves into the life of Sarah and looks at how the emotional roller coaster of childhood abuse impacted her physically and emotionally into adulthood. It dramatizes the long-lasting physiological and psychological impact of spending eighteen years under family duress. Children who grow up in chaotic homes learn to live in bodies that are always in a ready stage of "fight or flight," prepared to flee at any time with sudden changes in the behavior of those around them. Pediatrician Nadine Burke Harris describes in a TED talk that it is the "bear in the living room" syndrome. You always know the bear is there; you just never know when it is going to lash out at you.[3] Sarah became an internationally famous artist and this chapter describes her hard-earned ways to cope, overcome, and thrive professionally.

"Stop the Shame Spiral" presents specific tools that will help you break through your wall of doubt, teaching you how to stop the spiral of shame once it starts. Recommendations for personality characteristics to develop, based on my *Adversity and Success* research, offset the continuation of the childhood shame cycle. This chapter will teach you to appreciate yourself despite, and maybe because of, your childhood challenges.

This chapter provides a deeper look into how two different individuals manage problems at work based on the degree of shame they internalized when growing up. Luke comes from a healthy family and retains a strong sense of self despite problems at work, whereas Mary grew up with a strong sense of shame, which she carries into work situations. Feeling "different" as if there is something inherently wrong with you, or experiencing shame, is a consequence of childhood mistreatment. It can hold you back from seeking healthy relationships or cause difficulty rebounding from career detours.

"Build Confidence and Self-Esteem" explores how successful people have learned to bolster their self-esteem and confidence through a variety of techniques. Recommendations based on suggestions from the participants in the *Adversity and Success* research are outlined to give you practical avenues to improve self-compassion, confidence, and self-love.

In spite of her parents attempting to provide protection, love, and guidance, a situation outside of their control stole Sophia's self-esteem. Whether you experienced a specific traumatic event or ongoing family chaos, spending so much time in a self-protective mode leaves little time for developing a strong relationship with the *self.* This chapter gives practical suggestions to use in your personal and work situations to move your own self-confidence to a higher level. Use this chapter's core self-evaluation questions to gain a greater understanding of your own self-esteem deficits.

"Speak Clearly and Say What You Mean" helps you understand your core life values and how to communicate your values clearly. This chapter will not only help you identify your life values, but also develop skills to get your needs and wants met by strengthening your assertive voice. Assertive communication skills are critical to healthy adult relationships.

Ross, a high-level executive, whose father attempted suicide several times, discovered his values painfully at an early age through what he didn't like as a kid. Shannon, a managing partner at a large law firm, provides sage business advice on how to speak clearly at work.

"Give Me My Space – Establish Boundaries" describes unhealthy and healthy boundaries at home and work. It provides an assessment to help you evaluate your own boundary setting. You will also learn how to improve your skills at work to create strong relationships with healthy boundaries, fostering optimal cohesion and performance.

The real-life stories of Lucy and Paolina describe what they experienced as children, which then led to severe problems with boundaries as adults. Growing up in a home where individuals are not respected as separate beings, only as part of an unhealthy family dynamic, can create an unstable identity. When you can't adequately define boundaries, emotional confusion can arise over what is appropriate to say and do in relationships. In other words, you may subconsciously believe that you have to think like others to get along. Or you may feel like you have to always say yes and can never say no.

"Negotiate Conflict Well" In this chapter you will learn practical strategies for coping with intense arguments, quell your anxiety, and calmly engage with others until you have been truly heard and acknowledged. You will become more adept at fighting the "good fight." This chapter probes the extreme difficulty of withstanding workplace conflict by telling the story of Steve's struggle. People are frequently uncomfortable with conflict. They either freeze (deer in the headlights), flee the situation, or react with inappropriate aggression. Steve has owned many successful businesses, and his advice is based on over thirty years of solid experience.

More than half of the successful individuals I studied said they were comfortable arguing a point to closure. Being comfortable with arguments and helping others resolve conflict are essential skills not only at work, but for healthy personal relationships with siblings, parents, children, and spouses.

"Getting Out of An Unhealthy Relationship" Use this chapter's assessment to evaluate whether your current partnership is unhealthy or possibly abusive. A second assessment is provided to help you determine the impact of your marriage or partnership on your career and overall happiness.

The honest stories in this chapter dispel the myth that you can experience abuse at home and not have it affect the rest of your life. Gabriel's and Fran's stories show that you cannot easily reach your full potential while experiencing toxic relationships at home. Fighting repeatedly with a spouse who is abusive or alcoholic can cause damaging stress and drain the energy that could otherwise propel your education or career forward.

The **"Adversity and Leadership"** chapter delineates steps to gracefully get along with others, whether at work or at home are explained in this chapter. Compassionate accountability is outlined to help you handle specific situations in your life. You will learn how some business leaders overcame troubled childhoods to become transformational leaders, achieving high levels of respect and success.

This chapter tells the stories of David and Charlotte, both senior executives in their separate fields. David, possibly in response to harsh parenting, became incredibly successful and has advice for those wanting to overcome the same. Charlotte experienced minimal childhood troubles, which possibly limited her ability to identify the serious troubles her senior team was experiencing. This chapter clarifies how your leadership style can develop a culture that handles conflict in a direct, respectful, and healthy manner. This chapter presents insights into how leaders at a variety of companies and nonprofit organizations have successfully managed employees.

"Zoomers and Millennials Cautionary Tale and Recommendations" outlines descriptive research on how the pandemic impacted young adults, negative behaviors that harmed their health, and habits they recommend to help people thrive. These results are woven in with what experts in the field of building resiliency recommend to improve overall hardiness and to capitalize on one's strengths.

This chapter provides hope and inspiration by summarizing "turning points" for those who have experienced adversity and want to maximize their personal and work lives by capitalizing on their survival skills.

It examines the positive possibilities for survivors by outlining clear and actionable steps. During my experiences counseling and coaching clients, and through my research, I have learned that outcomes are greatly varied. However, as it was for me, a great deal of the power is in the hands of the survivor. To simplify what can be a difficult and confusing process, I have created a chart, *The Journey*, found in the appendix of this book, from childhood hardship to successful recovery, *The Journey* chart describes: the emotional and physiological impact of adversity; the personal and work consequences; skills and resources needed to heal; and attainable personal and work successes.

Become more resilient, tenacious, resolute, and happy. I want to help you turn your childhood and adult hardships into work and life success.

Grab a pen and let's get started!

Chapter 2
Identify Your Emotional Triggers

Our childhood experiences become an imprint of good and bad we carry into our adult lives. Our childhood sets the stage through the impact of adversity on our brains and nervous systems; trauma whether physical, sexual, or emotional, rewires the brain increasing emotional reactivity and decreasing our "governor." The amygdala heightens emotions, hippocampus interferes with memories, and the prefrontal cortex reduces effective management of our behaviors. In addition, nature or genetics accounts for 50 percent of our personality, but our childhood encourages certain biologically given traits to blossom or die depending on what is reinforced or squelched by our parents. In this chapter I will relate a work experience of Emma, a thoughtful and shy woman who was fearful of expressions of anger because in her family, arguments ended with broken objects, crying, and threats. She grew up being screamed at daily despite little provocation about almost anything. Her older brothers would rage at her as a way to cope with their stress. Fast forward to the age of thirty.

It was an incredible opportunity. Emma had unexpectedly secured a coveted position at a Fortune 100 company that employed scientists and researchers, fulfilled government contracts, and utilized state of the art manufacturing. But she grew up with parents who owned a small trades business and Emma was unfamiliar with corporate culture. She had spent the past ten years fleeing her childhood sadness and surrounding herself with thoughtful and soft-spoken co-workers and friends. In the nonprofit social service field, her co-workers had been respectful and mostly kind. She didn't expect the collision between her work style and those who would be her co-workers at the new job. She ended up working with people who were much harsher in their expressions of frustration and anger. She once again felt six years old and struggled to clearly communicate.

Emma was young to have obtained the amount of responsibility she was handed in her new position. She would be providing counseling and advocacy to a population of six thousand employees, half of whom worked in the factory and the other half of whom were researchers and scientists from other parts of the world. It was an incredible opportunity to practice psychology with her new graduate degree and license in a business setting.

Her supervisor, Jan, haltingly told her about the upcoming meeting with the union stewards to discuss the needs of the factory employees they represented. Jan mentioned they were an "intense" group. Emma had a sense of foreboding and anxiety more because of the way Jan told her about this meeting. It wasn't what she said—it was what she didn't say. This was a group of employees who had their fair share of chemical dependency, anger management, depression, and domestic violence issues. The screening and interviewing for many of these hourly positions was superficial due to the intense demands for quickly hiring to fulfill government contracts. Emma was the first person to arrive at the meeting. She wore a suit she had borrowed from her mom, new high heels that matched the suit, and styled her long unruly blonde hair to establish credibility.

The small conference room, although connected to the cafeteria, was cold. The ceiling was high and the chairs hard. Emma was the only one from Human Resources attending the meeting, which in retrospect, may have been an indication of what was about to happen.

The purpose of the meeting was to discuss how she would work with the union stewards and hourly employees to help them resolve work and personal problems. Emma shook hands and introduced herself to everyone. She was surprised, after working in nonprofit organizations, that only one other woman was in the room. No one was smiling or exchanging small talk. There were only stares and silence. Emma was acutely aware of how her attractive, blonde, blue eyed, and curvy appearance might be working against her. She had a long history of bad projections from men and women due to her appearance. But she told herself to focus and not get lost in fearful thoughts. She started the meeting by saying how excited she was to work at Honeywell and told them a bit about her background.

But no one seemed very interested. The lead union steward directed the meeting by demanding in a loud and threatening voice to know how she was going to work with Dick, the current counselor. Who the hell was Dick? No one had told her about him. She eventually gathered that Dick was a recovering alcoholic who had started working in the factory before being promoted to counselor. His job for the past thirty years was to help alcoholics and drug abusers into treatment programs. He didn't keep regular office hours but worked "the floors" during the week and by phone evenings and weekends to help families through all types of crises. His ultimate goal was to help individuals recover and stay sober. He was their hero, source of hope and loyalty.

Due to the yelling and swearing, it was almost impossible for Emma to understand what they were saying. Her primitive urge to fight, freeze, or flee was activated which made it challenging to concentrate. She tried to explain that she would be cooperative with

Dick but was slow to pick up on the severity of their concerns, seeing as no one had even told her about him in the first place. Eventually she understood that in their minds, her new position would jeopardize Dick's position and push him into early retirement. Emma tried to reassure them, but then realized the yelling and threats were just to put her on notice of their frustration, anger, and power. She was being bullied and was withering inside. As she listened, she felt like her ten-year-old self.

Emma found herself becoming very 'still,' as if she were a rabbit about to be caught in a trap; a freeze response. She wanted to hide from their wrath. She felt unable to speak. She had retreated to this emotional place many times as a kid when her brothers ranted at her for the smallest issue—how she dressed, her choice of friends, or not helping enough around the house even though she got up early every morning at the age of nine to clean the house before everyone else arose!

Emma eventually forced her way out of the rabbit hole and again reassured them that there was room in the company for both Dick and herself. She repeated, "We will work together and complement each other's capabilities." No one listened. They continued to yell, pace around the room, and swear to get their points across. She had walked into a battle that she would not quickly be able to understand or win. She finally gave up speaking and let them vent. At one point she thought she saw a bit of compassion in the expressions of one or two individuals who looked at her in a grandfatherly manner, but no one spoke up to calm this storm. Just like when she was a kid, she was on her own. Eventually they ran out of steam.

The meeting ended and people left without any summary of next steps to improve the situation. The stewards' presentation was not for the purpose of communication but was instead a show of power. Emma slowly walked to her office, gathered her belongings, walked past security and out to the parking lot to find her car. As if in a trance, she drove to the nearest McDonald's parking lot, turned off the car, and sobbed: deep uncontrollable sobs reminiscent of her childhood. The comments from the union stewards "got in her head" and she felt incompetent, doubting her ability to do the job. She questioned her right to have this prestigious position.

Emma called her mom and told her about the meeting in detail, received support, washed her face in the McDonald's restroom and drove back to work. She tried to appear calm and competent. Emma had been working long enough to know that it is critical to manage your emotions at work to be successful. No one would have guessed she was experiencing sheer exhaustion from "visiting her childhood at work."

Emma's Over-Reaction

What Emma didn't see going into this work environment was how different the culture would be from the nonprofit crisis and counseling organizations she had been a part of for the last ten years. In the nonprofit world, anger and aggression were expressed indirectly; there were strict unstated cultural standards for communication. She had never thought about how different communication could be outside of her profession and in a business setting.

It was a perfect storm. Emma had walked into a "work family" who had their roles, communication and hierarchical structure defined for the past thirty years. They were comfortable in their work identities. Their self-worth was securely attached to their positions. Most did not have college degrees, and Emma's new role as an employee assistance psychologist was forcing the other "family members" to question their self-images, responsibilities and how they related to one another.

As a child, Emma's brothers would yell, threaten, and hit her. They would continue storming at her for hours. And, now twenty years later, with her masters' degree and licensure in Human Resources, she was in the same position with an overwhelming amount of anger being directed at her. Emma's natural instinct from the biological flood of cortisol and adrenaline (stress response) was to shut down and flee. She expected herself to deflate, become little, and flee—therefore she did. Our expectations and beliefs of ourselves are powerful and self-sabotaging.

In spite of Emma's strong emotional and physiological reaction (she was flooded with stress hormones) to this stressful event, this was a pivotal moment in her career. It was her *opportunity* to harness her strong reaction and embrace this car crash between her past and her current reality. It was her opportunity to see stress as a way towards growth and increased resilience. Dr. Kelly McGonigal, author of *The Upside of Stress: Why Stress Is Good For You and How to Get Good At It*, explains, "The new science shows that changing your mind about stress can make you healthier and happier. How you think about stress affects everything from your cardiovascular health to your ability to find meaning in life. The best way to manage stress isn't to reduce or avoid it, but rather to rethink and even embrace it." The goal is to know ahead of time what might trigger a stressful reaction and then practice new ways of thinking and behaving to get better at managing it.[4]

Over half of the three hundred successful men and women I studied emphasized the importance of embracing and handling conflict at work well. Being comfortable with conflict resolution is critical for success. We all have situations that are stressful in our careers, but when you look back, the *intersection* of childhood experiences with the current reality determines our interpretation and how we behave in reaction to the event. Would the situation with the union stewards have affected another person as deeply as Emma? Probably not. Another person may have thought they were loud, blustering incompetents, not worthy of an afterthought. Clarity may be achieved by looking at this situation through a gender lens, however gender is only one small piece of the template from the past that we apply onto current reality. Would the union stewards have treated a new male psychologist in the same manner? Probably. Was it a bit easier for them to do so because of Emma being female? Probably.

We all get triggered in our adult jobs and emotionally return to the situations we experienced as kids. Our amygdala gets hijacked flooding us with emotions that are overpowering and lead us to say and do things that seem out of character and unprofessional. The key is mindfulness—to recognize that there are internal and external triggers that may be unconscious. Whether they are anticipated or unexpected, the goals are:

1. Become aware of what internal states or external behaviors overwhelm you.

2. Identify feelings and learn to tolerate them.

3. Learn new habits to harness your emotional hijacking.

4. Practice actionable steps that help you move towards more thoughtful behaviors.

The next day Emma met with her supervisor, Jan. Jan was a sophisticated and smart woman who had survived ten years of corporate life despite her own verbal lashings. She was in a managerial role and responsible for eight departments. Her job was to help new supervisors learn the skills needed to read financials, supervise others, and grow into top management material. She took her role of mentor seriously and was excellent at it. Jan provided clarification to the blustering stance of the union stewards and warned Emma about who could be trusted and what not to take too seriously. She listened and brainstormed to help Emma recognize when she was being triggered by a situation and to create strategies to manage conflict before there was an issue. Jan asked Emma, and I ask you—

How do you know you are being triggered?

Take a moment to write a few details about your own challenging home or work situations—how you felt physically and emotionally.

Home/Work Incident	**Emotions Triggered**	**Overreaction**
While I was making a point in the staff meeting, Joe interrupted and told me I was wrong.	Embarrassment Anxiety Shame	Stopped talking No eye contact
I returned home after a long day and neither my children or spouse acknowledged me.	Anger Anxiety Sadness	Started talking very loudly. Rudely told everyone to get off their cell phones.
Your experience:	Feelings:	Overreaction:

Hopefully, this exercise gives you some insight into how you are getting emotionally hijacked. Emotional hijacking occurs when a person is under stress and the amygdala, the part of the brain that regulates emotion, floods the body with cortisol and adrenaline, which overrides the prefrontal cortex, the center of thought and emotional regulation. You stop thinking and have strong, punch-you-in-the-gut type of feelings. If you have ever experienced an anxiety attack, you know the power of emotions to overcome rational thought. Let's look at some of the more common triggers and what successful people do to short-circuit them as they happen.

Emma's supervisor explained that there are common and expected triggers for most people. Jan encouraged her to become aware of her own triggers, accept that stressful events occur, plan a strategy to forecast the environment, and manage situations. Jan acknowledged that it is hard to change behavior as an adult but encouraged her to see the events as opportunities to become stronger and more resilient.

Check which of the triggers listed below are ones that are especially difficult for you to manage at home or work.

- ☐ Argument or conflict
- ☐ Competition
- ☐ Authority figures
- ☐ Irritability
- ☐ Loud voices
- ☐ Bullying behavior
- ☐ Swearing
- ☐ Touching
- ☐ Others' personal problems

- ☐ Narcissistic behavior
- ☐ Overwork or deadlines
- ☐ Performing in public
- ☐ Fatigue or illness

Creating new habits to calm your headspace regulates emotions such as fear, sadness, and anger; this is critical for coping with stress and trauma. Knowing what your own specific internal and external triggers are will help you read the environment and better manage your own emotional reactions before they happen. You want to have a blinding moment of clarity about what situations and behaviors send you reeling with emotion. Challenging situations create a physiological and emotional reaction, and it is important to understand how these emotions negatively affect your thoughts and behavior. If you have difficulty identifying your feelings, the *Feelings Wheel* created by Roberts, Tone, and Lieberman (2018) is helpful in labeling your emotions to be less reactive.[5]

Emma then turned the table and asked Jan the following difficult question. Once you identify you are being triggered, how do you begin to gain mastery over your emotional reaction?

1. **Observe yourself**. Notice how you feel when you are around certain people and in various situations. Look for patterns and connections between how you feel, your thoughts, and what you are experiencing. Write down what you are learning about yourself. Identify the people and situations that "trigger" strong emotions and radically accept that these automatic responses are a part of who you are. Approach encounters with your "surprising and least mature behaviors"

with respect, neither ignoring, avoiding, or attempting to forcibly overcome them. The goal is to learn what activates your past fears and insecurities before you are in a situation. Have an awareness of when you "feel less than" or when your "child" might become active.

2. **Reflect on the origins of your automatic responses – own them!** Radically accept where you are now with self-compassion. Focusing on your automatic responses with kindness allows for a better understanding of the past purpose these behaviors served. Understanding of how these automatic responses protected your vulnerability helps you loosen their hold. Acknowledging the origins of your triggers and radically accepting them is about owning all parts of yourself and standing in one place, paradoxically, allows you to choose new behaviors. By identifying your feelings and allowing yourself to experience them ,you become less reactive.

3. **Become aware of your automatic and undermining self-doubts** – your negative thinking. Learning cognitive behavioral techniques to challenge self-doubts can be helpful. It is not enough to just try to make negative thoughts about yourself go away; it is important to identify core scripts that you have internalized. Common childhood scripts are: I am helpless, I am unlovable, I am not worthwhile, and the world is a dangerous place. Harmful core beliefs cause interpersonal and mental health problems affecting an individual well into their adult years. Core beliefs are learned in childhood during stressful or traumatic times and seem rigid, but with practice they can be changed.

4. **See this stressful event as an opportunity to become stronger.** Being married, a parent, or having a career provides an opportunity to change—to become your better self and mature beyond your childhood fears and insecurities. Of course, it is not the other's job to help you change. It is your responsibility to tolerate the distress and communicate your beliefs and needs. Dr. Naomi Quenk, author of *Beside Ourselves: Our Hidden Personality in Everyday Life*, believes that an engaging and rewarding career can help reverse the damage of a bad childhood: "It is not uncommon for the demands of a career to force development and frequent use of our least preferred processes." Quenk encourages individuals to stretch and seek new work behaviors.[6] This concept applies to one's personal life also.

5. **Seek out opportunities to improve your awareness and try out new behaviors.** Overcoming your fears and insecurities creates excitement, hope, and resiliency. Observe and emulate others to determine which new behaviors are the best fit for your personality and communication style. Expand your repertoire of behaviors, like purchasing new tools for your toolbox. It is critical to develop the discipline to manage your emotions through repetitive behavioral efforts to strengthen new muscles.

I hope by now you realize that most of us struggle with changing our automatic reactions to stressful events. You are not alone. We often don't learn how to manage our emotions in our families, and yelling is commonly the reaction to a stressful event. All of us have strengths and weaknesses and increasing your well-being requires self-management. We need to remind ourselves, as Malcolm Gladwell, author of *David and Goliath*, states, "The powerful are not as powerful as they seem—nor the weak as weak."[7] We are all intimidated by situations and individuals, but do we need to stay there due to our childhoods? No.

Over half of high-achieving individuals had serious childhood adversity. They suffered sorrows and overwhelming chaos at times. Over a cup of coffee or a glass of wine, many men and women would confess their misfortunes and speak to me about the transformation of their lives.

They learned to manage their emotional reactions to become successful. Over 50 percent of the 310 high achievers I studied emphasized the importance of emotional intelligence and self-awareness as being critical to success. They also cited the importance of highly developed interpersonal skills and networking to understand and positively influence others. Many agreed that experiencing conflict is one of the most common triggers of extreme emotion regardless of age, gender, or organizational position. Over half of the successful people in my study said that being comfortable with conflict negotiation and staying at the table until there is resolution is critical to being a good manager. This emphasizes the importance of learning to manage our triggers to have a more mature persona at work. Throwing a computer against the wall out of anger will then be less likely!

Dr. McGonigal, author of *The Upside of Stress: Why Stress is Good For You and How to Get Good at It*, encourages others by stating, "Embracing stress is a radical act of self-trust: view yourself as capable and your body as a resource. You don't have to wait until you no longer have fear, stress, or anxiety to do what matters most. Stress doesn't have to be a sign to stop and give up on yourself. This kind of mindset shift is a catalyst, not a cure. It doesn't erase your suffering or make your problems disappear. But, if you are willing to rethink your stress response, it may help you recognize your strength and access your courage."[8]

To move forward, we need to accept where we are currently and understand that all our reactions and behaviors have served a purpose as we move through life. Dick Schwartz, Ph.D. in his book *No Bad Parts* encourages us to become familiar with our less preferred reactions and behaviors, to have compassion for ourselves and others to move forward. My study demonstrated that despite people on average experiencing two serious childhood events, when asked "How satisfied are you with your life, all things considered?" their response was *significantly higher* in satisfaction than the norm in the population. The results from my study found no association between a history of early abuse or alcoholism in the family and personal income, financial net worth, or happiness later in life. In other words, they learned from their childhood adversity, learned to identify their feelings, increased their awareness of their 'good and bad parts', and went on to manage their emotional triggers, becoming calmer and more thoughtful.

Chapter 3
Uproot Family Dysfunction

Your adult life is colored by your childhood problems. Adversity at a young age affects you emotionally, psychologically, and physically for the rest of your life. The world feels less safe and it is more difficult to have comfortable, healthy relationships at home and work. Yet, despite the original script for your life being written with adversity, these early troubles also create positive characteristics such as: *compassion, ambition, sensitivity, intuition, creativity, resilience, and grit.* The key is to understand how to take the disadvantages and have them work to your advantage.

Many of my very accomplished therapy clients initially have nothing positive to say about themselves; however, they overcame their problematic childhoods to become happy and successful. How did they do it? The first step in recovery is to understand how those troubles impacted you. I employed the Adverse Childhood Experiences (ACE) checklist in my most recent research which has been used with thousands of people to study the impact of chronic, unpredictable, toxic stress at a young age.[9] My results along with the results from other researchers, clearly demonstrate that poverty, neglect, and abuse are common, but have a significant impact on one's mental and physical health.

Forty percent of the 310 men and women I studied experienced one or more of the following as a child: 1) ongoing emotional or physical abuse—19 percent, 2) witnessed domestic violence—22 percent, or 3) had an alcoholic or substance abusing family member—24 percent (most often a parent). One in five of the study participants experienced two or three of these troubling events!

Surprisingly, they still reported a much greater sense of life satisfaction, owned businesses, went on to make an average of $250,000 annually, married, and had children. The average age was fifty-three—the youngest participant was twenty-four and the oldest was eighty-two. As adults, they reported multiple career detours and failures, but had a high level of resilience and flexibility. This group was significantly higher in the strength of their ability to socially influence others and to professionally network. The very troubles that made their childhoods unbearable at times appear to have made them tenacious and more resilient. How did this happen?

Children who grow up watching family violence or an alcoholic parent feel different than other children and their experiences *are* different. While others are at school focusing on their math or an English essay, these kids are distracted and worrying about what will happen when they return home from school. They may be anxious about a grade they received on a paper and whether they will get beaten. These situations sound extreme, but my research and the research of many others who study childhood adversity, shows that these experiences are incredibly common not just for women, but also for men.

Drs. Vincent Felitti's and Robert Anda's large scale ACE Study of seventeen thousand people demonstrated that childhood adversity resulted in a constellation of chronic conditions in adulthood. Children who experienced stress-inducing situations experienced a physiological shift in their stress response where it was set on high for the rest of their lives. They were more reactive to everyday stressors which then predisposed them to a host of chronic health conditions later in life.[10] Other researchers have demonstrated that kids who experienced the worst adversity made less healthy choices later in life, such as smoking and poor nutritional choices which led to obesity.

In addition, the first years of life are unequivocally important in determining which genetic hand you are dealt and will get expressed for the rest of your life. Your genetic predisposition for certain types of behavioral traits is either encouraged in their expression or discouraged and left to lie dormant.

For instance, if you were born with a tendency for neurotic anxiety, growing up in a fun-loving and relaxed family would decrease the intensity of the expression of that genetic trait. On the other hand, if you grew up in a family of conflict and instability, your anxiety would be heightened. Or, if you were naturally predisposed to alcoholism and grew up in a family where the parents did not drink, this behavior would not be reinforced at home. However, if you were genetically predisposed to become an alcoholic and your parents drank often and to excess, you would more likely become an alcoholic. This is called epigenetics—the expression of genes due to the environment.

The early years form our emotional and mental health. An obvious example is a child who is abandoned by their parent grows up feeling rejected and unvalued—not loveable. A child who hears yelling and objects breaking may end up being hyper-alert to tensions; he or she may have lots of anxiety. An anxious relationship attachment style is created setting a template for relationships in the future. Isolated incidents may or may not have a profound impact on a child depending on how dramatic they are, but daily and repetitive stressors may overload the child with the stress hormone cortisol. Dr. Kelly McGonigal, health psychologist, states, "Higher levels of cortisol can be associated with worse outcomes such as impaired immune function and depression."[11]

The consequences of abuse and abandonment vary widely and are affected by a number of factors including age and developmental phase of child, type, frequency, duration, and severity of experience, and relationship to the perpetrator. Child abuse and neglect can have long-term effects on physical health also, resulting in chronic lifetime health conditions. Impaired brain development in the areas of cognition, language, and academic abilities relate to mental health disorders. Children may adopt a persistent fear state as well as attributes like hyper-vigilance, anxious attachments, and behavior impulsivity. The stress hormones negatively alter the neuro pathways in the brain for the rest of their lives.

Psychologically, childhood adversity results in isolation, fear, and an inability to trust, resulting in lifelong consequences such as low self-esteem, depression, and relationship difficulties. How willing we are to get close to another person has a lot to do with our earliest relationships. Our interactions with our parents become a model for what we expect in future relationships. A child may develop avoidant or anxious attachment patterns extending into adulthood, pretending independence while being anxiously attached or being preoccupied with getting their needs met by their partner. The goal is to develop, through self-reflection and knowledge, ways to calm ourselves enough to have a secure attachment style.

It is the very juxtaposition of laughter and fun and screaming and abuse—where the two lines intersect with affection and hitting and the need for their parents' love and rejection that leaves scars. This ultimately requires "scar cream" year after year, never quite healing to the point of disappearing. What can be accomplished over time is to become more mindful to move ourselves towards happier and more rewarding relationships and experiences; this builds emotional self-discipline and positivity. It requires making different choices, practice, and repetition to squelch ingrained and automatic negative emotional responses and to work towards healthier and more positive ones. Think of it as learning a skill such as dancing or golf or a second language.

As I will discuss in future chapters, coping with adversity in childhood not only creates negative mental and physical consequences, but ironically can also result in adaptive behaviors that ultimately enhance one's life. Adaptive behaviors may include *wit, humor, self-reliance, self-reflection, determination, independence, and the drive to succeed.* The outcomes of childhood adversity are not all negative, which makes childhood problems more confusing when trying to resolve what happened as you were growing up. It is like the paradox of renewing connections that feel good at the funeral of a beloved friend. In addition, family situations are often not all bad, nor all good.

Examples of Abuse

To explain the principles of how your family adversity becomes internalized and affects you for a lifetime, I interviewed several people whose names I changed to protect their anonymity.

I asked a thirty-year-old woman, Nancy, about her upbringing and she described witnessing her mom being physically and verbally abused on a weekly basis. She said it was terrifying because of the uncertainty about how far the fights would escalate and the depression it created in her mother. Her mom mentioned suicide regularly. Nancy's high school years were marked by being at school and wondering if her mother would be alive when she returned home. The impact on Nancy included depression, lack of concentration at school, and social isolation. She also remembers being cornered in a bedroom with her mother repeatedly slapping her across the face. She appeared satisfied, seeing as "she deserved it" due to her misbehavior. Nancy also experienced ongoing verbal rage and abuse. She internalized her mom's disappointment and anger towards her, resulting in a life-long struggle with self-esteem.

I also talked to Joe about his father and how he would confine him in a dark room. At one point he beat him so badly he thought he was going to have to take him to the hospital. Fifty years later, Joe is driven to accumulate material things and succeed. He struggles with irritability and appropriate expressions of anger. He feels justified in expressing his rage if someone makes him angry and this behavior is reinforced by others because they go along with him even when they don't agree. He also feels calmer after an outburst. I talked with Greg, who was beaten by his father's Army belt every day after school until his kindergarten teacher came to the house and told his parents it had to stop. What could a five-year-old do to deserve such abuse? Nothing. The impact on Greg included a disregard for his own needs, dropping out of high school, and escaping at a young age into the military to put distance between himself and his parents.

This ongoing internal childhood stress creates a surplus of the stress hormone cortisol which puts kids into a perpetual "fight, flight, or freeze" state. Oftentimes, the kids truly do flee to the outdoors to walk and ride their bikes until there is no choice but to return home in the evening to face the 'bear' in the living room and hopefully to sleep. It is one thing if you encounter a bully at school and can leave at the end of the day and get a break, but when you live with the bully in your home and that tormentor is several times your height and weight, you are always in survival mode. The unpredictability of the living situation creates an extreme stress reaction. Children who grow up in a home with abuse and neglect may experience the following consequences:

- Impaired learning ability
- Academic problems
- Behavioral problems at school or with the law
- Weak social and emotional skills
- Lower language development
- Memory problems
- Inability to relax—fear, anxiety, insecurity and hypervigilance
- Depression and irritability
- Anger management issues
- Eating disorders
- Poor self-esteem
- Alcoholism and drug abuse

Abandonment, physical, sexual, and emotional abuse affect our bodies in several ways, including a rewiring of the brain altering the strength of emotions, memories, and ability to manage behaviors. There is a wealth of current research that now demonstrates trauma affects your brain's ability to function in the same ways it did before the extreme event. Trauma affects the amygdala, the hippocampus, and the prefrontal cortex. In other words, your emotions/instincts, your ability to form and maintain memories, and how you regulate your impulses and emotions are all affected. Experiencing extreme situations as a child creates a reaction as listed above that becomes part of your essence or core personality. When your body and mind are stuck in a state of fleeing, fighting, or freezing—a survival mode—it is difficult to process current circumstances. You are laser-focused on your escape. The happy carefree child you were meant to be never gets the chance to be expressed.

Not only is there a psychological impact to childhood sorrows, but there is often a physical result. Dr. Nadine Burke Harris, Ted Talk 2014, worked with the Center for Disease Control and Prevention and with Kaiser Permanente to study over seventeen thousand individuals, and the results are clear. Children who grew up with abuse in their homes or an alcoholic parent, holding for other factors, were more likely to have compromised health as adults, including heart disease, liver disease, cancer, obesity, high blood pressure, elevated cholesterol levels, and were more likely to die at a younger age. She sees familial abuse as a public health problem.[12]

I have friends who grew up in loving families where there was no abandonment, alcohol abuse, domestic violence or child abuse and the expression of their identities is different. They are calmer and more assured in who they are. Often, they have chosen marriages to their "best friend" and do not have dramatic scenes or ups and downs in their marriages. People who grow up in healthy families do not have pain as an integral part of their adult relationships.

This brings us to the question of how you move forward after experiencing childhood trauma. Even though 60 percent of the high achievers I studied experienced extreme problems as a kid, 90 percent of them reported *much higher* than the norm in life satisfaction. In other words, they were now happy. *How did they accomplish this and how were they able to move forward?*

Sarah Moved Beyond the Abuse

Sarah is a nationally known fine arts painter, and her story clearly illustrates the impact of abuse on the psyche of a child, which in spite of her clarity and creativity and success, follows her in life like a persistent flea into her eighth decade. Her works of art are deep, colorful, pushing the limits, and based in a broad definition of spirituality and international geographic history—Israel, Egypt, and China. She believes art is a way to make sense of the best of times and the worst of times. She states that she paints to understand life.

Sarah, tall and slim with an avant-garde style, grew up in a posh apartment in New York City. She was the youngest of three siblings and her mother was vivacious, charming, and beautiful. Sarah was truly blessed—or was she? Her Dad was also charming, intellectual, handsome, and was a teacher who eventually became the superintendent of the New York school system. Sarah's family was intellectual and sophisticated but expressed few feelings other than anger and rage. Her father did not want a third child due to the Great Depression, but her mother refused to have an abortion which sent their marriage into a downward spiral. Her father stopped having sex with her mother and her mother was angry! She sacrificed her sex life for Sarah. The marital dysfunction was passed down to Sarah and she expressed it through playing with dolls, poking their eyes out, and wetting the bed until she was five years old.

This caught the attention of her mother, who was frustrated and vacillated between finding activities to channel her energy and beating her. Sarah said, "She beat me a lot with a shoe and I had welts on my body. I would hide in a closet, but eventually had to come out. My brothers also hit me with various objects, and I felt like a victim. The beatings stopped when I was eleven years old. I was terrified as a child. My self-esteem was destroyed."

Sarah vividly remembers her father babysitting one evening when she woke up scared. She started to cry and cry. She was hysterical, but no one came to help her. She remembers being frightened and abandoned and feels she never got over it. She describes her parents as ambivalent, which led to a lifelong ambivalence towards herself.

Sarah's mom involved her in the art students league, and she sought solace in the Museum of Modern Art by visiting it over and over. Academically she did well and had the opportunity to choose between art and music. She chose art and said she paints to understand life and how the universe works. Sarah commented, "A family is never all bad or good. It is a mixture and that is exactly what is so confusing. The good and bad co-exist." Because of her environment and possibly her genetics, Sarah said she had several "nervous breakdowns," with the first one starting off as postpartum depression. She now realizes that she needs to take extreme care with her health and needs to sleep eight hours, eat well, and not take drugs or drink alcohol.

I asked Sarah if she thought her background contributed to her mental health problems and she said, "Yes. All my family was cold and intellectual, volatile, and ragers. Every night someone was yelling, and I was hit a lot—at least several times per week."

Kids who were physically, sexually, and verbally abused feel like there is something inherently wrong with them and even on their best days the simplest thing will trigger their discomfort. Sarah further explained, "I didn't fit into my family, felt like there was something wrong with me, felt unreal, was pretending and playing the role of good daughter, but was terribly lonely. I am now eighty years old and it has taken most of my life to come to terms with my childhood. I have done extraordinary things creating art out of historical middle eastern sites and I like myself most days. I am sweet, generous, authentic, have friends and a wonderfully supportive husband, but I still feel like a failure inside. I made the best use of my life I could. I still sabotage myself through helping others too much, but I have pushed and pushed myself most of my life. I have suffered and after you have been beaten, you beat on yourself. I attempt to heal myself through my work and also try to heal the world."

I asked Sarah what she recommends to others who have experienced childhood abuse and she said:

- Don't ever give up—practice daily self-care habits.
- Tell your story to someone who can hear you—a witness to your pain.
- Find what is meaningful that helps you get up each morning.
- Tell yourself the truth about who you are and work your ass off to be who you want to be.
- Don't look to material things and money for comfort.
- Find the right counselor and medication (if needed).
- Tune into your own body to discover what you need.
- Do mitzvah—good deeds to help others.

Jennifer's Relationship with Her Parents

In contrast to Sarah, Jennifer's life had a different tone and feel. Both Sarah and Jennifer were from upper middle-class families on the east coast with privileges most do not experience. However, the difference in parenting styles diminished Sarah's core evaluation of herself, making everyday accomplishments more difficult, whereas Jennifer's parents gave her what money cannot buy—love and respect towards herself.

Jennifer stated, "My parents loved us immensely and their intentions towards us were good. They were nurturing and affectionate. We always knew that we came first and had an important sense of participation in the family. They did not lavish us with praise but did something much more important. They expected us to help with dinner and other chores; therefore, we operated as one common family unit. Our responsibilities to be a part of a bigger whole gave us a mission and purpose. What we contributed mattered, and we received an allowance for our contribution. We were not spoiled and babied, but we were treated with respect. We were given responsibilities that increased over time commensurate with our age and abilities."

I asked Jennifer what happened when she misbehaved and she laughed and said, "I was nineteen and one evening did not come home all night. My dad sat me down and discussed the impact of this behavior on my mom and himself—his fears and his concerns. He taught me how my behavior impacted others while at the same time modeling respectful communication." They provided her with stability and predictable routines, combining secure emotional bonds with warmth and discipline.

Jennifer's family upbringing is by far healthier than others I have interviewed. However, there were some difficulties. She went on to say that her older sisters teamed up against her with harsh words and schemes to get her in trouble. She said they were incredibly mean daily. What is interesting is that the very solid platform her parents gave her helped her manage these troubles with her siblings without damage to her core essence. The problems with her sisters appear to have been just enough adversity to toughen her up for the adult world, but not so much to derail her sense of worth. She is kind and giving but knows when to stand up for herself.

Jennifer's parents soothed her, cared for her, and their care was predictable and secure. She said she has normal insecurities about aging in a very youth-oriented city. "But, in terms of who I am as a person and how I treat others, I feel good about myself. I like whom I have made a choice to become. I choose to be around like-minded people and never feel compelled to stay around if the person is not respectful and doesn't treat me well." She is self-confident and creates secure attachments with healthy people creating less dissonance in her "headspace."

Jennifer is competent, substantial, beautiful, smart, and well-educated. She has a happy marriage and successful children. However, that doesn't guarantee feelings of self-worth. Jennifer ended by saying, "I do love and respect myself." I think her parents did a damn good job and eliminated a long-term internal struggle that detracts from a happy and satisfying life.

How You Move Forward

Resilience, or the ability to maintain or regain mental health despite significant adversity, is a critical skill to acquire for adult well-being. Dr. Salvatore Madi, foremost researcher on resilience, has extensively studied how an individual can become more resilient. He recommends the following steps:

1. Increase your personal control by consciously making decisions and expressing your needs and wants.

2. Enhance your connectedness to others by devoting time to the people you choose.

3. Discover the meaning and purpose for your life through examining your values.

4. Develop hope and positive expectations.[13]

Other "resilience" researchers demonstrate that many people routinely overcome various kinds of early-life obstacles, loss, and trauma to become more resilient later in life. Resilience and hardiness experts describe a stress inoculation effect that helps individuals cope as adults when faced with further adversity. They emphasize that adult strength is acquired through managing earlier childhood problems. So, how do you get there?

Are You an Adult Who Experienced Childhood Adversity?

The first step in your recovery process is to identify and acknowledge whether you experienced trauma as a child or young adult. The following is a summary of the Adverse Childhood Experiences (ACE) checklist. If you have experienced even a couple of the following, you have experienced childhood adversity:

- Swearing, insulting, humiliating, or behavior that made you feel like you might be physically hurt?
- Pushing, grabbing, slapping, or throwing something at you? Ever left physical marks?
- Touched or fondled inappropriately?
- Feel as if no one loved you, took care of you, or thought you were important?
- Often hungry, wore dirty clothes, or had no one to care for you or take you to the doctor?
- Lost a biological parent through abandonment, divorce or death?
- Witnessed your mother being pushed, grabbed, had something thrown at her, hit repeatedly or threatened with a gun?

- Lived with someone who was a problem drinker?
- Lived with a household member who was depressed or mentally ill?
- Experienced a household member going to prison?[14]

If you have experienced any of the trauma listed above, it is time to start your healing process and you are probably wondering how to do so.

Focus on Your Strengths

Just as your environment can enhance "God given" characteristics, your genetic gifts such as intelligence, athleticism, verbal acuity, attractiveness, height, and strength or emotional characteristics such as kindness, determination, and independence can all help you overcome and thrive despite your oppressive upbringing. Let me give you an example. A young boy, John, who is physically and emotionally abused daily by his parents, engages the attention and protection of one of his teachers due to his intelligence. His athleticism garners the attention of his coach to the point where he plays in every baseball game and his grandma attends every game. His independence gains him a job on a ranch during the summer months where he earned money to get himself out of the house and away to boarding school.

Focusing on your strengths and developing them further can create a pathway to well-being and success. The following steps can help you use your past as an opportunity to grow, work towards greater self-acceptance, and achieve happiness:

1. Acknowledge and radically accept the adversity you have experienced.

2. Know your values and make choices that are in alignment.

3. Learn the language of feelings

4. Identify and limit maladaptive coping behaviors such as overeating, drinking, gambling. pornography and shopping that provide a quick dopamine "fix."

5. Approach your challenges with compassion and kindness.

6. Practice daily self-care habits that calm your mind, such as, exercise, eating healthy, meditation, prayer, hobbies, and seek out respectful friendships.

7. Practice conscious control of your emotions through mindfulness techniques.

8. Learn cognitive behavioral exercises: identify your core scripts about your worth to help you reframe what you repeatedly say to yourself.

9. Develop hobbies and skills to calm yourself.

10. Pursue a meaningful career and work towards success.

11. Seek counseling and read self-help books.

12. Rewrite your own story to emphasize your resilience, growth, and the meaning of your experience.

Rewriting your story is critical because if you tell yourself and others repeatedly your childhood story and emphasize only the negatives, you are "cementing" it into your emotional and psychological being. This intensifies the childhood emotions and fuels your quest for understanding and a nonstop loop of the bad things that happened. When you grow up with constant conflict and disrespect, your emotions propel you to more vividly and frequently remember only the bad experiences. The intensity of the negative emotions, plus the need to understand what happened turns into a negative loop that is harmful. The more that incident(s) is recalled and ruminated about, the more it becomes etched stronger and stronger in your psyche. It is like a patch of weeds that take over the flower garden of your life.

Literally rewriting your story allows you to more freely experience the happy times in a safe environment—to fully experience the ice-skating competition success, the soccer game win, or time with grandparents without fear of retribution or anxiety. Rewriting your story allows you to:

- Gain clarity on what family themes have been passed down from generation to generation that you don't choose to carry.

- Release positive emotion by identifying any happy or calm experiences.

- Focus on positive achievements, relationships and experiences.

- See your whole life for what it is without being overshadowed by the negative experiences and emotions.

- Clearly identify what you have accomplished and who you have become in spite of your hardships.

Running from our problems does not help, but standing in place and radically accepting our challenges with compassion creates an opportunity to grow. Rewriting your story with an eye to your strengths and success slowly changes the negative childhood template. Try it!

Stop being embarrassed and "own" your experience. It has made you who you are. You can love your parents and not like their behaviors, but admitting to yourself the severity of the impact of your upbringing can provide you the freedom to move on. You had these experiences, and nothing can change that; therefore, you may as well ask yourself, "What is the learning in this for me and what can I take forward to improve my future?"

How we deal with our trauma defines us. Anyone who has been through trauma as a child has an overabundance of empathy and compassion for others, which can be used in a positive way when enough time has passed. Once one gets through that trauma, he or she has the opportunity to do great good in the world.

It may take a while to figure out what your gift to the world is, but it is there. Would Sarah have become such an extraordinary painter without her childhood struggles? Would I have become a psychologist and helped hundreds of people heal from their pasts—probably not. Our greatest emotional wounds spur our unique and precious gifts to the world.

Keep "stepping off the ranch" into new territory and learn new behaviors and habits to calm your demons of self-hate in your head. Learning to cope with childhood and adult sorrows and understanding how they can define and hone our strengths can result in greater self-understanding and compassion—this is the adversity advantage.

Chapter 4
Stop the Shame Spiral

Shame is the feeling that there is something inherently wrong with you. We all carry shame, which can make our interactions with others personally and professionally awkward and difficult. Painful childhood experiences can make us believe we are flawed, unworthy of love and belonging. At its essence, shame feels similar for most people, but for those who grew up with abuse, alcoholism, or poverty, the need to keep the secret from others magnifies the feelings of shame. Outward manifestations of shame are lack of eye contact, flushing, stunted verbal communication, poor posture, and poor hygiene and self-care.

The emotional environment of the family in which you grew up plays an important role in how much shame you internalize. Grandparents pass on regrets and shame to their children who then pass on the shame they feel to their children. The family unintentionally provides a context for getting stuck in shame, especially if there is poverty, abandonment, abuse, or alcoholism. Shameful parents raise shameful kids, and it is passed down similarly to anxiety or depression. Shame becomes the rope tied around an individual that keeps them from being their authentic self and ultimately exuding competence and caring for others. However, you can have positive control over how you identify situations that increase your shame, how you think and talk to yourself, the interpretations that you assign to your experiences and how you react to them, and the choice to love yourself.

My research on success and well-being clearly showed that authentic relationships and building a social support network are critical to well-being and effectiveness at work. Strong relationships and social support also are an effective way to overcome shame in your personal life.

Seventy-five percent of the successful people I studied experienced one or more difficult events as a child, including poverty, death of a family member, divorce, school problems, bullying, alcoholism, and physical or sexual abuse. They described feelings of worthlessness and low self-esteem as a result of these problems. They also kept their family secrets, which led to shame. They internalized the verbal abuse thrown at them and believed they caused the abuse because they were told that something was wrong with them.

The unanswered question is: if I was worthy, wouldn't these adults have noticed I was sad, alone, abused?

Luke—Not Much Shame

Luke returned home from work, uncomfortable and acutely aware that he did not handle a meeting with a new customer very well today. He chose to go to the baseball game and had a few beers the night before (had a great time) but didn't get home until late and only slept about half as much as he needed. Therefore, today at work he was groggy and more abrupt with his peers. He lacked energy and an important new customer could tell he was off his game. The meeting moved along without much enthusiasm and ended with a lack of clarity about who was going to do what as next steps. He was certain his co-workers rolled their eyes at one point when he couldn't answer an obvious question. Luke's breathing became quick and shallow, and he couldn't think clearly—his flight response was activated. He was the main contact with this new contract, and it was his responsibility to handle things well. His primary contact at the other company ended the meeting by saying, "So far I am unimpressed by your lack of organization." Luke was afraid they were going to initiate the thirty-day cancellation clause.

After the meeting, Luke went back to his office and in spite of feeling shameful about his sub-par performance, he said hello to a couple of his co-workers and shook hands with a new employee. Even though he wanted to close his office door, he left it open, responded to a couple of requests from the people he supervised, and then decided to call it a day. He put a smile on his face and walked to the parking lot.

Luke started to ruminate about his competence and then exercised his self-discipline and self-compassion—told himself to stop. He did not want to spiral down into a vortex of shame. Luke utilized self-discipline and was determined to only let himself review the facts. He did not allow himself to make the situation into a catastrophe by assigning more meaning than it deserved. He calmed himself by remembering how often he handled crises at work and how well he got along with his co-workers. Luke utilized healthy "self-talk," telling himself, "Yes, you screwed up today, but you can't be perfect every day at work. You shouldn't go to a baseball game late, nor drink during the workweek, but I guess you had to remind yourself of that lesson." He made a plan. "I will go to bed early tonight, get some rest, get to work early tomorrow, and call the customer to clarify the next steps to implement the program."

Luke turned off the lights and went to bed and did exactly as he told himself to do. He learned from his experience, but didn't waste time berating himself or letting the mistake make him question his competence or worth.

Luke's reaction was a healthy response to making a mistake. He went in to work the next day, pulled together a quick meeting and reached out to his colleagues, acknowledging to his co-workers that he should have been more prepared. He then apologized. Luke took responsibility for the difficulties in the meeting and had the courage to speak his mind, thus modeling solid communication for his work group. By doing this, he connected with others and increased the meaningful and authentic relationships he already had. Luke modeled vulnerability, which took courage, and his co-workers expressed empathy in a variety of ways.

Luke came from a family where each individual was respected and valued. He did not grow up in a family full of shame and could demonstrate steadiness more easily during a storm. His parents provided him with love and consistency—a strong base for good self-esteem and self-love.

Workplace Culture

So often our workplace reminds us of junior high, with all of the belittlement and back-stabbing we experienced as teens. Our interactions at work aren't that different at times. Our bosses make us irrationally angry, our co-workers betray us behind our backs, and we sometimes say things that we can hardly believe came out of our mouths. Whether you're dealing with difficult bosses, uncooperative co-workers, or being disappointed in yourself yet again, you are likely to say to yourself: "I feel different, like there is something wrong with me." This kind of statement reflects upon how you feel about yourself right now and if it is, it oftentimes holds you back in your career and personal life every day. The culprit is called shame.

However, that's not the only problem. Given how common shame is in daily life, you or your co-workers are very likely to have grown up in a home where everything was uncertain. You (or they) may not have known whether during breakfast, spilled milk might set off yelling, throwing things, name calling and shaming. Because parents are everything to their children, the damage is likely to be severe when the parent verbally abuses the child with such phrases as: "What is wrong with you? Why are you wearing that outfit? Are you trying to get boys to look at you?" Or, "Why are you crying? Be a man. In my day we went to school all day and then worked until the sun went down. You have it easy. You have no stress and no problems! What is wrong with you?" The child does not have the mental capability and strength to say, "There is nothing wrong with me, but there is something wrong with my parent!" Since parents rule that child's world, the child eventually starts to wonder, "What is wrong with me?" and carries that shame into adult work life. Your co-workers also bring their potential for shame into work. What complicates this further is that some work cultures are based on shaming employees to get tasks completed and to achieve better results. However, many employees do not see another option for employment, while others stay because the shaming feels familiar and isn't identified as being unhealthy. The workplace simply mimics the shaming the employee received while growing up in a family of adversity and unhealthy behaviors.

Mary—Lots of Shame

I just gave you an example of Luke, who was from a healthy family. The level of shame he internalized was minimal. Mary, one of his co-workers, had a different experience on the same day. She gave a presentation to a group of two hundred managers and supervisors about the implementation of a random drug-testing program. What she did not anticipate was the negativity in the audience about the subject and the very specific operational questions that were going to be asked. The managers who supervised both hourly and salaried employees wanted clarity on the process, legalities, procedures, timeline—all of the implementation details she did not have yet. What was different between Mary and Luke is that Mary walked into the conference room with lots of shame about herself. She grew up being berated and physically abused. When the audience started angrily asking her questions she could not answer, she gave up and turned the talk over to one of her co-workers. Shame had overcome her. She experienced a strong urge to flee. Instead, she froze, could not make eye contact, felt like she had gone down a rabbit hole and didn't know how to turn around and come out! She could have been honest and said, "There are lots of details and procedures to work out here. I will work with the Human Resources Department and will have that information to you in two weeks via email and then we will have follow-up brown bag lunch seminars in small groups so you can get all of your questions answered." However, overcome with shame, she lost her ability to think and speak.

Mary went home that evening and cried. She felt inadequate and embarrassed. When she looked in the mirror, she was disgusted at what she saw. She never felt "good enough," questioned whether she herself was a mistake, and didn't want to return to work. She tossed and turned throughout the night, ruminating about what happened and fearing discipline. The thought of facing everyone seemed an insurmountable task. Mary's experience triggered her shame, and she lost her perspective. Yes, she had a very bad work experience, but it did not mean she was a bad person. However, she felt like a complete failure and didn't share her experience with her partner. Mary went to work the next day, but avoided people and stayed to herself, wearing her shame like a badge. This did not help her, nor did it help her department fix the problem.

Most employees go to work with varying amounts of shame in areas including intelligence, verbal acuity, appearance, and likeability. When work cultures have problems, often it is because there are self-esteem and shame issues that get inflicted into every work communication, decision, and meeting. Have you had an experience where everything you try to discuss with a co-worker becomes awkward, difficult, and fraught with emotion? It is very possible both parties are experiencing shame in reaction to one another. The end result is a lack of work cohesion, productivity, and cooperative goal setting.

Larry's Shame as a Supervisor

Take for example a mature scientist, Larry, who has been directed to work with and supervise a young employee named Ted. Larry is regarded as brilliant at his job but has not progressed very far in management. He has his own shame issues about his interpersonal skills, ultimately limiting him at work. Ted is seen as a natural expert in getting people to work together but is generally viewed as less intelligent than Larry. Ted, aware of this, has had awkward interactions with Larry from the beginning. Neither of them is aware of how their own shame is unconsciously triggered by the other. Larry feels like a failure with people and Ted feels shame about his inexperience. Despite their efforts, progress is not happening, and their work deadline is looming.

Finally, Ted stated, "Larry, I am not seen as the brightest bulb on the block and frankly I am surprised I even have this great position." This honesty was refreshing and made them both laugh for the first time. Ted continued, "But our deadline is approaching quickly, and I need your help in figuring out what we should present. I can't do it without you. I need your expertise." Ted overcame his shame and was authentic in asking for what he needed. Larry reluctantly replied, "Well, you are good with presentations." He admired Ted's honesty and vulnerability and stopped being a disagreeable supervisor. Moving past shame allows us to build relationships, seek opportunities, rebound from the detours and failures we all experience, to be flexible, and stop ruminating about our inadequacies. The ability to do these things was listed by the high achieving participants in my research as "avenues to success."

My aforementioned *Adversity and Success* research identified important skills for supervisors to master including:

- Strong communication skills
- Emotional intelligence
- Decision-making
- Team building

The skills listed above are not possible with shame being activated on a regular basis. The way to ensure a strong competent presence is to identify which employees and situations are more likely to make you feel shameful and to do your personal work to make sure that you stay calm and confident. The next section has specific suggestions on how to break through your wall of shame.

Breaking Through the Invisible Wall of Doubt and Shame

Life is difficult enough without carrying around an internal sense of embarrassment about who you are, and wondering what you did wrong after each disagreement or debate. Shame drains your energy because so much time is spent covering up and protecting the fragile image of yourself to others. However, that is exactly the way it is for many co-workers because almost half of us have experienced trauma as a child. That wasted energy could be used in more productive ways. Shame at work can have dire consequences on your career. It can limit your networking and social capital, which is necessary for success. Building good relationships with your peers and getting along with your boss is important for being promoted. Use the following tips to pull yourself out of the vortex of shame in those moments when all you can think of is your inadequacy.

- Be mindful—become aware and accept your thoughts and feelings in the moment.
- Familiarize yourself with what shame feels like for you.
- Recognize your silent "internal shame script" of self-criticism.
- Write down your positive traits and keep the list visible.
- Write down your positive attributes and say positive things to yourself.
- Remove yourself from negative situations.
- Try to use humor to defuse the situation.
- Make a connection with someone you care about.
- Repeat a saying that calms your mind and emotions.
- Focus on the next thing you need or want to do.
- Have unwavering compassion for yourself.
- Remember the bigger picture and what you are trying to achieve.

We all have moods of despair where we berate ourselves with resultant feelings of emptiness and worthlessness. Dr. Brené

Brown, in her book, *The Gifts of Imperfection*, recommends four ways to make yourself more resilient against shame: 1) name it, 2) talk about it, 2) own it, and 3) tell your story.[15] This sounds easy, but when you are an adult and feel like a vulnerable child, it is difficult to reach out to someone else and discuss your pain and sense of unworthiness.

In his book *The Science of Happiness*, Dr. Stefan Klein helps us to not take our own internal dialogue too seriously by explaining that the brain seeks out stimuli that match our emotional state. When we feel anxious physiologically, we seek out anxious thoughts. We spin inner dialogues—our "silent script"—that keep us prisoner to our shame. He recommends getting the silent script of "arbitrary and unconscious judgments" down on paper to raise your awareness and change your thought processes about yourself.[16]

Chatter: The Voice In Our Head, Why It Matters, and How to Harness It, by Ethan Kross examines the ongoing conversations we have with ourselves and how it shapes our lives. Kross provides tools to help calm your headspace including mental time travel, changing the view by being a fly on the wall, imagine advising a friend, reframe your experience as a challenge, normalize your experience, and distancing yourself from your self-talk. It is necessary to try out a variety of tools to find ones that work for your specific personality. All tools build and strengthen new muscles to calm your headspace.[17]

Personality Characteristics to Overcome Shame

My *Adversity and Success* research showed a very clear pattern for men and women who were victims of childhood chaos, such as familial abuse or alcoholism. The men formed less close personal relationships at work and the women were involved in less informal social activities at work, thus demonstrating a more protective interactional style. Being less open to work relationships and having less social capital may adversely affect one's career. Certain individual personality characteristics correlate strongly with success at work. Conscientiousness, following through while paying attention to detail, is extremely valuable. This specific characteristic is not a problem even when one is immersed in the shame spiral. In fact, it may provide some relief to intensely focus on a new task to get away from the feelings of shame. Nevertheless, the next four characteristics are important to keep in mind because they are not only associated with success but are difficult to express when one is consumed with shame.

Extraversion, openness, low neuroticism, and *agreeableness (flexibility)* are characteristics required to develop to have a stronger presence at work. Right after an incident that triggers the strong emotional and physiological response of shame, reach out to others (extraversion), try a new behavior that is unusual for you (openness), consciously decide to focus on and write down what you did well (low neuroticism), and instead of being rigid and defensive due to your shameful fear, be flexible to another's request (agreeableness).

By keeping in mind the personality characteristics of high achievers and working towards the development of these skills, when shame gets triggered, you will shorten the shame spiral and move on more quickly. Despite their childhood misfortunes, both the men and women I studied were resilient and flexible to accommodate and prevail over commonly encountered career detours and failures. These individuals frequently started their own businesses in spite of growing up in shame-based families. Sixty percent of the people I studied were courageous enough to start their own businesses, possibly due to their difficult start in life, as if to say, "No one is going to be the boss of me."[18]

Overcoming Shame and Anguish

I asked the men and women I surveyed how they were able to overcome such a troubled start in life to find internal peace. Here are some quotes from the group:

- "I surrounded myself with positive individuals—rather than those who increased my self-loathing. For instance, my older siblings always laughed and made fun of me, which made me feel foolish. Once I moved away from them I met individuals who viewed me as someone with lots of potential and encouraged me to ask questions and push the limits of life. I far exceeded my wildest expectations, when my husband suggested I return to college." *Performer & Composer*

- "See your adversity in perspective and relate your current strengths to early adverse situations you chose to overcome!" *Healthcare Executive*

- "I think you must figure out what your gift is as early as possible. Everyone has a gift but we try and force ourselves into positions that don't serve us well, If you figure out what you are good at, position yourself in a role that sets you up for success, the self-confidence comes naturally. *Vice President Sales*

- "Understand yourself. Do not fear personal analysis and allow your weaknesses to become strengths." *Director of Hospitality Services*

Your shame may have been passed down from your great-grandparent to grandparent to your parent onto you and then down to your children. However, this is one family secret and legacy that you don't have to perpetuate. Decipher the power of the secret by rewriting your story and break through that invisible wall of doubt and shame.

Chapter 5
Build Confidence and Self-Esteem

Certain work styles contribute to success and translate into a happier personal life. Extraversion, conscientiousness, creativity, determination, authenticity, and communication skills all lead to successful outcomes. However, what if for the first five, ten, or fifteen years of your life you are subjected to unpredictable chaos? Maybe you grew up in poverty not knowing where your next meal would come from or whether your parent would be sober. You possibly lost a sibling, and no one had the wherewithal to help you through this personal trauma.

Our self-worth is damaged when we are abused and neglected. Our self-worth is also the single most important factor in determining our happiness and success at work and in our personal relationships. Therefore, it is critical to work towards greater self-esteem to ease your path in life. Over half of the highly successful people I studied experienced very serious childhood problems and they went on to create better and happier lives.

All of our experiences during childhood affect our adult work life. Poor self-esteem is a drumbeat that never quiets. How do you build social capital when you are afraid of the opposite sex? How do you grow authentic relationships when you hate yourself? *Feeling good about yourself and having confidence is essential for building strong relationships and accomplishing new challenges.* When an individual lacks self-confidence, everything is more difficult—personal relationships, work relationships, and seeking and meeting new challenges. Self-confidence is needed for traversing complicated situations arising from difficult bosses, unpopular work assignments, short deadlines, too few resources, handling discrimination or sexism, developing relationships with the opposite sex, honing a professional way of speaking, and grooming your personal appearance. Accomplishing difficult tasks one by one will improve your self-confidence, but that takes time. Self-esteem and confidence problems take a long time to develop and, therefore, it takes time to change ingrained thoughts and behaviors.

While it is not the purpose of a company or job to help employees heal from childhood difficulties, I am a firm believer that a meaningful and successful career can help heal the most basic and primitive wounds for a healthier adult life. Work groups are a new family of sorts and experimenting with new behaviors to achieve more honest and authentic relationships with co-workers can help immensely. Accomplishing new and difficult tasks, achieving success, and being rewarded for it helps heal wounds from the past and also increases feelings of worthiness and confidence.

Confidence is a combination of feelings and behavioral habits that interact together to help you be more effective in life. If you don't feel confident, you can use confident behaviors to help you feel stronger. Also, the opposite can be true. If you feel confident, but are slouching or mumbling in front of others, you appear and may feel less confident.

Confidence at work and life in general is everything. People can sense whether you are confident or not and will treat you accordingly. My research, *Adversity and Success*, identified core self-evaluations of high-achieving men and women by using the Core Self-Evaluation Scale created by Drs. Judge, Erez, Bono, and Thoresen.

This reliable and valid standardized questionnaire included items such as:

- Overall, I am satisfied with myself (self-esteem).
- When I try, I generally succeed (self-efficacy).
- There are times when things look pretty bleak and hopeless to me (neurotic negativism).
- I determine what will happen in my life (internal locus of control).[19]

The 310 men and women I studied, despite their severe childhood troubles, were both significantly higher than the normative population in their core self-evaluation. They liked themselves and believed in their ability to make a positive impact on their own lives in a way their values dictated. They were able to overcome this rough start in life to become confident adults and to maintain high self-esteem.

While most of the *Adversity and Success* research showed more similarities than differences between the women and the men, there were two interesting exceptions. First, the men had higher core self-evaluation ratings than the women even though they had similar problems as children. Second, although the men reported as much childhood abuse and family alcoholism as the women, the women who were abused as children reported many more problematic consequences of their childhood troubles as adults. Compared to the men in my study, the women specifically reported:

- Lower life satisfaction (still higher than the norm)
- Lower self-esteem (still higher than the norm)

- More divorces
- More likely to give in when arguing a point to closure
- Experiencing prejudice due to their physical appearance and age
- More business ownership

It is possible that the men went beyond their comfort zone in admitting the amount of trauma they experienced as kids and therefore were not willing to go into detail about the long-term impact on their adult lives. Many researchers today still believe that abuse is only a women's issue; however, it is not. As many men as women in my study were impacted by family abuse. Many of the men who witnessed domestic violence between their parents stated that they helped more at home with their own families and felt more compassion at work for struggling employees.

There can be other positives from the adversity you experienced as a child. It is painful to think about, but it has made you into the complex individual you are today. The high-achieving men and women I interviewed said childhood troubles made them more:

- Compassionate towards others who are struggling
- Patient when others have problems
- Determined
- Self-reliant
- Resilient[20]

Paradoxically, for many abused "big kids," their childhood misfortunes have made them more kind and patient toward others at home and at work, but not necessarily more confident on a daily basis.

Even When Parents Do Everything Well

Sofia is a fifty-year-old Hispanic woman. She is an accountant, beautiful, kind, quiet, and competent. Tragedy in her personal life forced her to come to terms with her lifetime struggle with a lack of self-confidence. After twenty-five years of orchestrating everything—house, lawn, children, cars, and finances—she unexpectedly lost her husband to a heart attack. Sofia had relied on her husband socially and had withdrawn from others due to her weight gain. They filed for bankruptcy for his business after two years of difficulties. After her husband's death, Sofia made the decision to move to a less expensive home, sell his belongings and build her business of private consulting to support the family. There was nothing to fall back on financially—no savings or life insurance.

Sofia sought counseling for herself and the kids and redirected them back into college. During the last few years of counseling for herself, she realized that she lacked self-confidence. She had been comfortable taking a back seat to her affable and adventurous husband and charismatic, athletic, and smart children. Doing most of the household maintenance while working part-time enabled her to avoid confronting her problems with confidence and weight gain. It became a downward spiral because she was overwhelmed with the house, kids, and work and therefore snacked throughout the day to cope with stress. Without her husband, there was no longer any buffer between herself and the world. After a couple years of being a widow and working from home, Sofia decided that she was too isolated and preferred having work colleagues. She applied for several jobs and to her surprise, each one was offered to her.

Even though she had been raised with well-educated parents—her father was a dermatologist and her mother was a dentist—she suffered from low self-esteem and low self-confidence. Her parents were kind, steady, and supportive and there was no abuse or alcoholism in her family. However, when she was seven years old, her parents went to France for several months and her grandmother took care of Sofia and her toddler siblings. Three seventeen-year-old boys, friends of her older brother, took advantage of the situation. They initially bribed Sofia into her father's car in the garage with little wax bottles of juice and then sexually molested her. The fear this generated in her was tremendous. She knew it was wrong and wanted it to stop; however, the teenage boys threatened her by saying they would kill her beloved cat, Tiger. The young men molested Sofia frequently for several months. At one point, they hung a dead black cat, similar to Tiger, from a telephone wire in a tree in front of her house to make the threatening point clear.

Sofia said, "I didn't say anything to anyone for a long time and when I was nineteen, I told my sister, who then freaked out and told my parents. My parents were very upset, flew to my college, and then told me they both knew about the sexual abuse! I was even more devastated, felt betrayed, and I flipped out. We had a huge fight. My parents said they had consulted child psychologists around the country who suggested they just watch me. However, seeing as I had friends and was getting good grades in school, they thought I was fine." There was a long pause and she continued, "What they didn't know is that I was cutting myself and it helped to release the emotional pain I felt. I absorbed the sexual abuse and anger and internalized it against myself. I experimented with drugs to numb myself against the secret I carried and the anger from the abuse. I also gained weight in college and began a rigorous schedule of exercise by running twice a day for several miles. I would count five carrots, which was all my food for the day. If I also had celery, they couldn't touch each other. I still have this odd habit today. At the time I was becoming an adult, I was starving myself. Eventually, I sought help for my eating disorder with a college counselor who was very helpful. She was the first in a long line of therapists who helped me."

After another pause, Sofia quietly said, "Of course I forgave my parents. I have forgiven everyone involved, but I do not talk to my older brother. I wish it didn't happen, but there is nothing I can do about that. Once you experience abuse, it is a part of your makeup—a scar. It is part of who I am and everyone has something. It has made me a stronger person and I survived it. People love me even though they know; it reinforces that I am okay and that it was not my fault."

I asked Sofia about her self-esteem. "I have lacked self-confidence and self-esteem. Even though I am very accomplished, I feel dumb. With all the resources in my family and the education of my parents, I could have become a veterinarian, which would have been my dream. I know that my lack of self-confidence and self-love is related to the sexual abuse I experienced."

She has struggled with depression and is grateful to have had a wonderful twenty-five-year marriage and two loving kids. There is a huge discrepancy between how others see her intelligence, personality, and beauty and how she sees herself. Like many of those I interviewed for this book, Sofia has a very low profile and is comfortable being alone—a more self-protective style. She is very kind to everyone and has a few close friends. To calm demons from the past, Sofia highly recommends the following to empower yourself:

- Daily exercise to reduce stress and boost endorphins
- Outdoor activities to be in nature
- Practice mindfulness techniques, including meditation to increase awareness

- Develop assertiveness skills to express your needs and wants
- Supportive and authentic relationships
- Counseling

She is a wonderful mother, has a very protective instinct towards her children, and pushes for open dialogue. Her purpose and overarching mission to nurture and protect her children became intensified due to the sexual abuse she experienced. It was not until her husband died that she proceeded with counseling to work through her own grief and realized her life-long struggle with self-confidence. During counseling, she was able to determine her core values and find the energy for self-care. She realized that she had lacked self-confidence most of her adult life. Counseling helped her to understand how the sexual abuse undermined her self-confidence for most of her life.

Today, Sofia has lost fifty pounds of fear, insecurity, and low self-esteem. She has learned about mindfulness and gratefulness, which has enhanced her life. She is working full-time in an accounting firm, supporting the family, exercises intensely five times per week, and is dating. Sofia is confident and optimistic about the future, perhaps for the first time in her life.

Work and Self-Confidence

It is the rare individual who does not struggle with self-confidence at some time. Relationship challenges, new jobs, speeches, illnesses, aging, and other challenges cause us to pause and doubt our capabilities. Situations where we need to perform in front of others, and especially when demonstrating a new skill or knowledge, is often when confidence becomes unsteady. Insecurity is different for everyone. Your lack of confidence will be directly tied to the experience you have in what is being asked of you. For instance, if you are a great communicator and have worked hard to develop those skills, speaking to your work groups about potential downsizing won't be as difficult for you as it could be for others. On the other hand, describing the financial reports for your division may send your stress level soaring due to your lack of expertise with numbers. It is essential to know what you are comfortable doing and what subjects or tasks cause you anxiety. Often people feel a lack of confidence in the following areas:

- Public speaking
- Appearance
- Speech, including grammar
- Intelligence
- Knowledge
- Lovability

Admitting to yourself how your personal past is impacting your career today is essential to moving forward professionally. Options to move forward include getting a coach, seeking out employee assistance services, attending seminars, reading self-help books, or finding a professional counselor.

In my first study of successful women and men, a clear pathway to success was described. The following behaviors and attitudes require confidence. This is what the surveyed self-made millionaires and multi-millionaires recommended:

- Communicating well to socially influence others

- Being confident and authentic
- Openness to creativity
- Managing conflict well
- Work engagement
- Perseverance and resilience to overcome obstacles
- Developing honest and respectful relationships
- Team building
- Using humor
- Lower level of neuroticism[21]

There were a few important gender-related differences in the pathway to success. Sixty-five percent of the women I surveyed said they experienced frequent sexism on the job. I have worked with some wonderful men as peers and bosses and I interviewed some of them for my last book, *The Millionaire Mystique*. Ninety percent of them stated there are specific career obstacles for women. Over 50 percent of the men said leadership was different for women than for men. Over 35 percent of the women who were business owners, CFOs, and CEOs said they tried to look less feminine at work. The women also most often handled the "second shift" in the family even when they were primary breadwinners. When women were in leadership positions, expectations were for them to handle their responsibilities like men. These gender-related challenges require a stable level of confidence and esteem to negotiate effectively.

The goal is to maintain a baseline of confidence, so new and difficult experiences don't stop you from feeling good about yourself. Many people today say, "Fake it until you make it" and while this is good advice for minor jitters, it won't take you far if you have long-term self-confidence issues. Confidence, a belief in your own ability—your own self-efficacy—is one component of overall self-esteem. Building self-esteem on and off the job will decrease the anxiety in your life overall and make everything easier to navigate. Increasing your self-confidence will help you to be less neurotic and worrisome. So, how do you do this?

First, become aware of your tendencies to magnify, jump to conclusions, and personalize bad situations. Often our negative thoughts become a self-fulfilling prophecy. Take the time to write down your negative and irrational thoughts because we rarely see our own distortions. And, then follow these suggestions.

Quick Tips

- Focus only on the task at hand.
- Write down what you are telling yourself about this task—negative thoughts.
- Replace negative thoughts with positive ones you truly believe.
- Calm yourself through a brief meditation, relaxation exercise, or prayer.
- Write about your fears, what could be the worst outcome, and how you would deal with that outcome if it happened.
- Model others who are competent.
- Over-prepare—plan ahead.

Problems with self-confidence are not created overnight, but developed through years of interacting with playmates, family members, teachers, and sports teammates. Therefore, building self-confidence involves ongoing, consistent effort over a period of time:

- Take a moment to assess your areas of self-confidence—write them down.
- Identify the people or situations that undermine your self-worth on a daily basis (pay attention to how you feel around certain people).
- Practice new behaviors to expand your repertoire.
- Take care of yourself physically with nutrition, sleep, and exercise.
- Understand the "secondary rewards" that may be pulling you to practice behaviors that undermine your confidence (e.g., cookies taste good but make you gain weight, or staying in a bad relationship because you find security in it).
- Recognize and replace self-defeating thoughts—gently and repeatedly.
- Develop the habit of self-affirming and positive thoughts.
- Practice love and compassion for yourself in spite of imperfections.

Confidence is a constellation of life experiences, competencies, and a belief in yourself. Developmentally, as you age and have some of those life experiences that knock you back, such as divorce, illness, or financial difficulties, you may struggle with your self-confidence similarly to when you were younger. It is as if the current stressor triggers old behaviors and feelings. At these times, be patient with yourself and practice what centers and strengthens you. Know that this difficult time will pass. Above all, be compassionate with yourself—there are situations and times for all of us where even though we put forth our best effort, feeling confident is a tenuous struggle.

Confidence Assessment

1. Write down situations or skills where you feel confident.
2. What are the positive messages you received about yourself as a child?
3. What people and situations make you feel less confident?
4. What are the repetitive feelings and thoughts that arise in challenging situations?
5. What are the negative messages you received as a child?
6. What behaviors can you start now to improve your confidence level?

You are probably getting a pretty good picture of how and why your life has diminished your self-confidence and optimism and how it still affects you today. Positive adult relationships, work achievements and accomplishing goals can be healing, rewarding, and a road to greater self-esteem. Success in relationships leads to a greater level of self-confidence and personal fulfillment. Building skills and negotiating new relationships, challenges, and opportunities, leads to a greater overall sense of confidence and self-esteem at home and work.

Chapter 6
Speak Clearly and Say What You Mean

It takes courage to be the person you really are and it can be difficult to figure out your authentic voice. It may be most evident when you are drifting off to sleep at night or waking in the morning. Most of the day, our defensive minds spend time trying to ward off feelings and knowledge about ourselves. In the evenings and mornings, we are most vulnerable to our vital truth. It is also more difficult for people who have experienced poor parenting or hard fortune as kids to know and define their values and to have the communication skills to express their individual needs and wants.

Living with family chaos day in and day out requires so much attention to protect one's self and to stay safe. The best the child can do is "cope." He or she is managing fear, anxiety, sadness, and possibly depression. Usually, the family invests great energy into keeping its secrets and anyone who spills those secrets to the outside world experiences severe consequences—including being told they are wrong, crazy, and a "traitor." Obviously, with this much chaos in a home, values are not discussed, and children are not helped to identify and understand their own beliefs and desires. The communication styles they have witnessed are often highly dysfunctional and damaging. As a result, young adults have their own truth delayed, not to be discovered until they are away from the incredible stress and dysfunction of their family.

Winning Friends and Influencing Others

In my *Adversity and Success Study*, the men and women emphasized the importance of being socially astute, developing rapport easily with others, and always instinctively knowing the right thing to say or do to influence people to enhance their lives. This highly successful group rated higher in the characteristics of openness to others and agreeableness (flexible and forgiving). Higher than the norm political, interpersonal and networking skills correlated with life success. In other words, developing the skills to transform your life from one of unexpressed feelings, needs, and wants to clarity of communication in order to influence others is essential for contentment at home and work. How do you reach these goals when you are from a chaotic family that communicated poorly?

No matter what your age, it is never too late to be true to yourself. You know you are embracing your true self when you:

- Feel balanced and have positive energy
- Actively choose when to be in a relationship
- Are not dependent on others' opinions
- Have an internal locus of control—an internal direction
- Speak honestly without guilt
- Know your value is innately within you—not due to wealth or material goods

Ross – Man of The House at Ten

I worked with Ross for ten years for a start-up company owned by a Fortune 100 firm. We all worked incredibly long hours. The stakes were high and the stress intense. We either became profitable or the subsidiary would be shut down. Even though we were in the business of helping people, our profit margin was critical. Twenty years later, I called Ross to ask him if he would be interviewed for this book because he demonstrated an unusually positive way of "managing" his peers and had a way of speaking his truth that was genuine and direct. This communication style added to his effectiveness and our overall success. Little did I know that his social skills were attained in a very painful and difficult manner starting when he was ten years old.

Ross specializes in marketing and sales and has held high-level positions in many start-up companies. He is currently focusing on a company that helps others live their best lives through education and counseling. Ross's dad was bipolar during the years when the field of psychology didn't know what to call it. His strongest childhood memory was when he was ten years old and the ambulance came to take his dad to the hospital because he had attempted suicide. Ross said, "I knew this was very bad and I felt sick. But I didn't have the skills to process what was exactly happening." This was the moment when his mother started to rely on him as the man of the house. She was involved in outside activities such as the PTA but had checked out of the family emotionally. His dad attempted suicide every five years until psychology caught up with his illness and his psychiatrist prescribed lithium. His dad was in adult full-time mental health care for many years. Ross remembers one incident when his mother had been in a car accident. His dad, wanting to help, went out and in a manic episode bought two new cars they could not afford. Ross, as an embarrassed teenager, had to return both cars and try to explain to the salesperson about his dad's mental illness. His mom packed her bags many times but stayed unhappily in the marriage.

Lithium was effective for Ross's father, who had four years of freedom from his emotional anguish. During this time, he was very helpful to others with mental illness. However, he smoked six packs of cigarettes a day and eventually died from lung cancer. Ross watched how others treated his father over the years and he identified two responses—pity and rejection. He never wanted to treat others in either of those ways and believes how his mother and others treated his father pushed him at a younger age to identify his values on how best to be in relationships.

Ross is grounded in the concept of grace—God's unearned love and favor for everyone. Ross said, "Everyone needs grace and acceptance. I was confirmed in the Lutheran Church and its basic tenets helped me identify my values and truth. I decided how I wanted to treat others regardless of the situation."

Ross gave his first sermon when he was thirteen years old. It was a ten-minute sermon about grace and forgiveness. His pastor helped him write it. Ross grew up in the church, which gave him very clear values. He was not only busy with church but was president of the student body in high school. He worked full-time starting when he was fifteen all the way through two college degrees. Interestingly, he says he always had good self-esteem, was at the top of his class, and had a very high IQ, which his high school journalism teacher confirmed. She insisted that the combination of his high IQ coupled with hard work would make him successful. Ross continued, "I was driven to help my dad feel pride and to give him something to live for—sometimes to my detriment. I was always trying to achieve more."

A pivotal experience for Ross came when he finished the seminary at age twenty-four. He was required, along with the other students, to complete a ten-week intensive clinical program to explore his own issues before helping others. He had a wonderful counselor who was brutally honest. His counselor helped Ross identify that he was very angry at the world for how his father was treated.

Now that we know the origins of Ross's emotionally intelligent communication style, I asked him how he applied this to his life. He has hired, supervised, and fired many employees and suggests the following **communication principles:**

- Approach every interaction with others with grace and acceptance.

- Try not to take exchanges personally.

- Be in constant dialogue about how an employee or co-worker is doing and give specific feedback.

- Be honest, otherwise you are working under a false premise and the person won't be successful.

- Tell the person that you have their best interest in mind, you want them to be successful, avoid confrontation, present the facts, and be genuine in the way you communicate care.

- Communicate what you have observed and hold up a mirror to the other person.

- Focus on solutions to improve performance.

- If you need to fire someone, provide directions to help with their resume or job search.

In summary, Ross wisely states, "Most people are unaware of their own behaviors and blame others. Hold yourself accountable for your response. Of course, life is not fair, but what is important is what you do with it. You can live life in the shadow of trauma or look deeply inside to find your truth and let go of the pain. You cannot rewind the tape. You won't forget the anger and sadness, but you can forgive. Ask yourself what in your past or present is preventing you from living your best story? What is it going to take for you to live your best and true story?"

With humor Ross concluded our interview by saying, "How many counselors does it take to change a light bulb. One, but the light bulb has to want to change! Look in the mirror!"

Ward and June Cleaver

Shannon's parents were like Ward and June Cleaver on the 60s T.V. show *Leave It to Beaver*. She is a managing partner at a large and prestigious law firm in Phoenix. Shannon said that she grew up in a family with parents like 'Ward and June Cleaver.' There was no fear of retribution or obstacles in giving opinions or talking at the dinner table. There were four kids and they all participated and felt heard. Shannon felt smart and valuable. The six people around the dinner table taught her at an early age to speak up to be heard. In the sixth grade, she told everyone she wanted to be an attorney. No one said she couldn't be one because she had the best grades in the family.

Everyone accepted it as fact that she would become a lawyer one day. While Shannon described her upbringing as positive and supportive, she did explain that as the third child she was often the brunt of teasing. She remembered being sensitive and crying easily at times, but often she would hold her own with her older siblings. The dinner table debates appeared to be just enough adversity to toughen her up for the world of work, but not so much that she couldn't articulate her needs and wants.

Shannon is still sensitive as an adult; however, being an attorney allows her to engage in a heated debate with specific parameters. Her true adversary is the attorney representing the opposing client and she is comfortable fighting for her clients. She is successful and well-respected for her calm and kind demeanor in the community.

Even though Shannon is a managing partner in her large law firm and very successful, she struggles when confronting employees over poor performance. She stated, "I am too non-confrontational. It is very difficult for me to deliver difficult and negative messages. The difficult times are when I have to tell someone they did not become a partner or I have to fire them—tough messages to deliver when I am crushing their hopes. I try to be in constant dialogue with the employees I supervise by giving positive and constructive feedback continually. I have a tendency to dodge the really difficult conversations, but once I do it, it is not that bad."

However, Shannon does not have a problem speaking her mind at home or work and recommends the following sage **advice** for clearly communicating at work.

- Reflect on the politics and players in the organization. Determine the best way to have your comments heard.

- Refuse to be dragged into negative conversations and competition. Rise above it and be mature.

- When providing constructive criticism for a performance evaluation, seek coaching and make a plan of action with human resources.

- Develop your cognitive and emotional intelligence.

- If someone doesn't like your behavior, keep in mind that it is their problem.

- Compartmentalize communication problems at work, so you can get a good night's sleep.

Both Ross and Shannon have provided great communication advice for personal and work problems based on a combined fifty years of management experience in high-level positions. However, if you are still unsure of what communication style is right for you, let's focus on some questions to identify your values around communication. For instance, for me, yelling at others and being yelled at are against my core values.

Speaking Your Truth in Your Way

Ross makes the process of identifying and speaking authentically sound easy, but from his story you know this was learned through a lot of pain, hardship, and self-reflection. If you grew up with severe troubles as a child, there are important developmental tasks that you missed. The first step is to identify and understand your own values. Values are guides or behavioral standards for communication and are influenced by our families, individual experiences, religion, culture, and our communities.

Life Values

Knowing your values is the basis for communicating clearly and making good decisions. To gain a greater understanding of your top values, check off from the following list:

____ Love

____ Family

____ Spirituality

____ Safety

____ Success

____ Creativity

____ Exercise

____ Friends

____ Power

____ Health

____ Leisure

____ Wealth

____ Knowledge

____ Achievement

____ Education

____ Beauty

____ Nature

Once you have identified your top values, it is important to ask yourself whether your life is structured in such a way for you to focus on these values. In other words, if education is a top priority value, have you allowed yourself the time and resources to pursue further education?

Communication Values

Not only do we have values that build structure for our lives, but we also have values for how we want to communicate towards others and how we want them to communicate with us. Forty percent of the group I studied grew up with explosive communication, including yelling, blaming, and name-calling. This can result in an overly protective and socially withdrawn communication style at work or passive aggressiveness. To further understand your values around communication, answer the following questions. Check those that apply.

1. What are my most important values around communication?

____ Respect for others

____ Calmness

____ Honesty

____ Compassion

____ No swearing or name calling

____ Humor

____ Caring

____ Reason

____ Clarity

____ Appropriate expression of anger

____Wisdom

____ Fairness

____ Knowledge

2. What communication behaviors do I most dislike?

Check those that apply.

_____ Yelling

_____ Crying

_____ Swearing

_____ Mumbling

_____ Blaming

_____ Vagueness

_____ Ignoring

_____ Condescension

_____ Stone walling

3. Identify someone you know and respect: role model their communication style. What behaviors do they have you would like to emulate?

4. How do you build time in your schedule to create authentic communication with those in your life?

5. How do you regulate your emotions and calm your headspace when facing problems?

If your communication style is in line with your values, your communication with others will be clearer and more effective. Poor communication at home or work will diminish your individual effectiveness. Poor listening creates indecision and harms relationships. In addition, integrity and honesty also were highly recommended for success by my research participants.

In an unhealthy family, values are not clear and there are often mixed messages between what is being said and what is done. An example is someone who says he values conscientiousness, but doesn't go to work and loses his job. Or, someone who proclaims to value managing her temper well, but loses her temper regularly. In unhealthy families, the rules change according to the demands of the people in power without any warning or logic. On the opposite end of the continuum, healthy families have clear values that act as a road map for everyone to follow—no lying, no cheating, and demonstrating respect for one another.

Communication Skills -Active Listening

Communicating clearly is a challenge for many of us and when you are ill, tired or stressed, it becomes more difficult to clearly articulate what you want to say. At these times, basic active listening skills can be very helpful. Active listening involves:

1. Being an attentive listener,
2. Maintaining appropriate eye contact,
3. Paraphrasing to show you understand,
4. Asking open-ended questions,
5. Body language consistent with your verbal message,
6. Speaking clearly and concisely,
7. Demonstrating empathy and concern,
8. Conveying respect for others' ideas,
9. Appropriately giving and receiving feedback,
10. Entering conversations with a flexible and open mind.

Possessing strong communication skills will reduce your stress at home when talking with family members and at work. Communicating consistently and authentically in accordance with your values provides you with a calmer headspace. What keeps us from finding, acknowledging, and acting on our truth? Busyness. Comfort. Fear. Identifying your values, knowing when you are being true to yourself, and developing strong communication skills are the keys to a more rewarding and congruent life.

Chapter 7
Give Me My Space—Establish Boundaries

Personal boundaries are rules or limits people create to identify how others may behave towards them and how they will respond if someone oversteps those limits. Boundaries serve to protect someone emotionally, psychologically, and physically. Healthy boundaries establish independence and autonomy from being controlled by other people's problems, feelings and thoughts. In healthy families, kids learn how to do this at an early age.

How do you know if you need to improve your boundaries? Nedra Tawwab, author of *Set Boundaries, Find Peace*, lists the signs that you need to improve your boundaries.

- You feel overwhelmed.
- You feel resentful toward people asking for help.
- You avoid phone calls and interactions with people who might ask for something.
- You make comments about helping people and getting nothing in return.

- You feel burned out.
- You frequently daydream about dropping everything and disappearing.
- You have no time for yourself.[22]

Growing up without clear boundaries at home can result in not having appropriate boundaries as an adult with co-workers and friends. Relationships become burdensome as professional boundaries are blurred. This makes it more difficult to relate to others and creates poor communication and unhealthy relationships.

When kids don't learn healthy personal boundaries at home, it is more likely they will not have good boundaries at work. An example of a boundary violation could be—you are at a party and someone you do not know well approaches and puts their arm around you while talking. Even though there are others at the party, you feel uncomfortable, hyper-alert, tense, anxious, and distracted. You tell yourself your feelings are silly, but it does little to quell your emotions. These feelings are a sign that your boundary has been violated. Examples of boundary violations I have personally experienced include being:

- Patted on the head
- Patted on my pregnant belly
- Pinched on my posterior
- Asked repeatedly about my personal life because I was single
- Told I didn't need to make a good income because I didn't have children

- Followed off the highway into the work parking lot

- Stared at during meetings

Boundary violations happen in all organizations. As an executive coach, I have not only witnessed men violating the boundaries of women, but also seen women regularly crossing the boundaries of young men who work for them. There are many ways to have bad boundaries at work. A supervisor with poor boundaries creates many problems for himself and for the group as a whole. You may find yourself listening to an employee's personal problems every day to the point where you cannot get your work completed, or you might get involved in office gossip, date a colleague, or become overly involved in an employee's personal decisions.

Boundaries as an adult are more problematic for individuals who grew up with their boundaries being violated every day at home. Boundary violations take the form of being screamed at, sworn at or abused physically or sexually. Dysfunctional families often have enmeshed boundaries, where the child's actions are experienced by the parent as an extension of themselves. The child is not seen as a separate individual with his or her own personality, talent, skills and needs. Roles may also be flipped where the child of an alcoholic or a child who witnesses a mother being abused may take on the parent role and care for the adult parent as a way to cope. It takes a long time to realize that taking care of your adult parent at the expense of yourself is really a way to desperately ensure your own safety as a kid—very sad, but true. Big 'adult kids' who grew up in chaotic families often have a high tolerance for poor behavior and need to learn how to have firm boundaries.

This chapter contains accounts of successful, happy adults who worked hard at self-discovery, overcoming adversity, and defining and communicating their personal boundaries to ensure that what is happening around them is safe and healthy.

Lucy's Road to Recovery

Lucy grew up with a chemically dependent parent and poor boundaries. She is a very athletic, attractive and personable psychologist in Des Moines, Iowa. She has three children and has been married for twenty-five years. She was one of ten kids growing up, and as an adult, struggles to maintain healthy relationships for herself and her family. When I asked Lucy about personal problems, she states that she has been a huge enabler, not holding others accountable for their behavior. The enabling interfered with her success and a professor asked her if she was from an alcoholic family as she was trying to control a whole project group to no avail. It was then she made the connection between caretaking and control. It is a fine line. She added that for many years in her career she accepted crumbs in the form of lousy hours, poor pay, bad offices, and the most difficult and unrewarding projects and clients.

As she described her childhood adversity, she focused primarily on the divorce of her parents when she was four years old. There were only two other kids in the whole elementary school who had divorced parents and she felt "different" and singled out. Her dad was an alcoholic and went through treatment twenty times during the marriage and after the divorce. Her mother, like many other women in the sixties, turned to the church for marriage advice. She was told by the priest that it was her duty to stay married because marriage was a sacrament, and it was a sin to get divorced. If a marriage was annulled in the seventies, the kids were then "bastards." Even though the kids were constantly screamed at by their dad, hit with a belt on bare bottoms, and slapped in the face—"it was chaotic; it was crazy"—the church said it was a sin to get divorced.

Lucy's mom was a devout Catholic and after selling a restaurant and getting a large amount of money, she donated it mostly to the church. Her mom's whole life was dedicated to the church, but eventually after getting her husband, Scott, into chemical dependency treatment again, she got a divorce. She was told by the priest that she was a disgrace and could no longer receive communion. Lucy's mom was forced to choose between her religion and the safety and protection of her kids.

I asked Lucy how she coped as a child. She said, "There were neighbors in my life that were supportive and caring. They would show joy when I would visit and tease me and call me 'Miss America' and 'smarty pants' in a positive way. My grandparents were also solid role models, which helped me to become more resilient." Lucy's childhood was spent volunteering—for the church, for the hospital, meals on wheels, raking for the elderly, youth ministry, and many other different organizations. Helping others was a way the whole family coped with their adversity. As a result, she wanted to be a nurse. She would go to the Shriners Hospital with her uncle, an orthopedic surgeon, and see the very sick children. She admired how he handled life and death situations with the kids and gave them hope.

Lucy described the family volunteerism as extreme and incredibly invalidating to anything the kids experienced in their own lives. No self-care was taught.

In college she identified an eating disorder in herself—she vomited as if she was trying to expel her past and exercised two to six hours per day in order to be thin. She said she was obsessed with how much she weighed, how much she had eaten that day, and how much she had exercised. She stated, "My eating disorder robbed me of minutes, hours and days. For twenty-five years I was held hostage by it." She eventually went to the University of Iowa's Counseling Center and received help.

Lucy said she had obsessive compulsive disorder, and everything had to be clean and orderly. She jokingly stated that she should have worked for United Colors of Benetton because she loved to organize her sweaters by color, and everything had to be folded perfectly. Control is a common characteristic for kids who grow up with chaotic abuse and alcoholism in their families—it is an attempt to gain control over their environment due to anxiety.

Lucy learned to be very accommodating, enabled others and always did the lion's share of the work whether at home or college. She came across as controlling, which was a way to prevent and cope with chaos. She confides, "You don't go into the field of psychology by accident. I was trying to work out my family history." Her personal enabling sabotaged her career when she didn't follow through on her scholarship to become a minister. She was too distracted by family problems. In addition, Lucy was imminently distracted by her fairly new marriage and children. She regrets not becoming a minister and wonders if there would have been a way to combine both into her life. Not surprisingly, she chose to put others first and finish school quickly.

Lucy reflected on what got her through so much family chaos as a child. She remembers escaping to the outdoors, biking, camping, sports and reading. She spent hours outside kicking, hitting, and chasing the ball with friends in the neighborhood and siblings. Instinctually, she pursued her passions—the things that nurtured her soul with a driven spirit.

What Worked for Lucy

Lucy has been very successful in creating a positive family life, rewarding profession, and is a "best friend" for many people in the community. She has broken the cycle of abuse and alcoholism with her children, who have graduated from great colleges, are spiritual, fun, and have good moral character. Lucy chose a profession that, indirectly, also helped her recover from her chaotic and abusive childhood.

As a psychologist, Lucy had a supervisor who practiced the "competency based" model of therapy. She was told that if you were only trained to look at problems, it would bring the client down further. She was directed to see the competencies in her clients and therefore began to see competencies in herself. One of Lucy's competencies was to view situations from a research and sociological/anthropological perspective. In many different positions in healthcare, she wrote protocols, policies, and procedures for the rest of the departments. She understood childhood abuse, parenting issues, eating disorders, and alcoholism. Lucy was passionate about helping other counselors handle cases well. Her obsessive-compulsive behavior lent itself to creating very specific procedures on how to treat clients. Do you understand how she turned her maladaptive childhood coping mechanisms into career strengths and how you might do the same?

Lucy recommends the following strategies for self-care to move beyond your childhood problems:

- Develop your faith and spirituality (*most important*).

- Focus on your competencies.

- Learn compassion for yourself.

- Identify and emulate five people who are good at self-care.

- Understand the things that hold you hostage—thoughts and behaviors that were necessary for survival as a kid that are interfering with your success as an adult.

- Seek counseling with someone who focuses on positive psychology, not just pathology.

- Read self-help books.
- Have a 'go to' mantra or prayer.

Lucy ended our conversation by saying, "There is not a short and easy route to recovery from poor boundaries. It is an arduous, painful, circuitous, and lifetime journey. Nevertheless, the journey can be highly entertaining and rewarding if you are a seeker of knowledge about yourself and celebrate your progress."

Paolina's Pivotal Moment

What was especially confusing about the sixties and seventies is that in many families with underlying problems, the surface looked respectable to the outside world. For instance, Christmas was complete with a real tree, decorations, homemade cookies, lots of family gatherings, and presents carefully wrapped under the tree. Homes were decorated with colorful red, blue, and green lights to reflect the merriment of the season. Many of us believed in Santa Claus way past the age where it made sense. Mothers had more traditional roles working only within the home and most of the needs for the home and children were well taken care of. However, the freedom afforded the fathers, sometimes coupled with alcoholism, affairs, and abuse created a harsh contrast to the mother's life and made the dysfunction even more confusing to the kids. One of the negative results of kids living in conflict is that they may feel overly responsible for others, be extremely emotional, and be enmeshed—have poor boundaries between family members. In other words, everyone would feel everyone else's feelings.

Paolina described her Christmas: "I received lots of my desired presents for Christmas, but more often than not Mom would not talk to Dad, therefore everyone would be anxious. We grew up and became stronger because we survived family problems and developed skills to take care of ourselves, which we would not have had to do if our childhood conditions were easier."

Paolina grew up in a family of five kids. She was the oldest and said, "I was an adult at ten years of age." Her parents were young, fun-loving, and attractive when they got married at twenty-two. She went on to say, "My mom vomited all over us kids with her negative emotions about my dad. He was a big drinker and my mom was Sicilian, where emotions always took precedence over intellect." She described her dad as a "fun drunk," always gregarious and charming. People loved to be around him—people outside the family. He was handsome with dark hair and eyes that twinkled with mischief. He especially loved Christmas, when he would lavish gifts upon them to make up for previous problems. Paolina says she could not understand why her mom was so cold and angry after receiving a beautiful watch from her dad, but now knows they were placating, apologetic gifts for the damage his drinking had done.

Paolina understood quite a bit more when she had her own collision with her dad's excessive drinking and her own disappointment. Paolina was seventeen years old and went to the father-daughter dance at her Catholic high school. She was excited and wore her favorite party dress. They had a lovely dinner, exchanging conversation with the other father-daughter duos. She was proud of her handsome and friendly dad. However, after dinner he started pounding down the martinis one after another. She wondered if he had forgotten that she was there. He became louder and louder with the other fathers and Paolina grew more quiet, embarrassed, and ashamed. She wanted to disappear into the comfort of her bedroom.

Paolina's mom had told her for years not to drive with her father after he had been drinking, so she called her mom to come pick her up. She left her dad at the bar. The next morning, in his usual way, he was gone early to travel for work before she woke up.

After Paolina had started college, her dad—on her mother's demands—went to the Henry Ford Treatment Center for chemical dependency. Her mom dragged all five kids to family seminars and sessions in order to understand the impact that chemical dependency has on the whole family. Paolina sat with her younger siblings listening and trying to understand how her father's drinking and her mother's codependency had impacted all of them.

This very act was a pivotal moment and indisputably changed the rest of Paolina's life. This was her corrective course of action. She learned about healthy boundaries, how to express needs and wants, and to set limits with others. She evolved and learned not to put herself in the middle between her mom and dad. Paolina's dad stayed sober for a few years, but eventually her parents divorced.

Her newfound skills were put to the test ten years later when she became engaged. Paolina handled things very differently due to the counseling she experienced in the past. When choosing a partner, she said, "I asked myself what I liked about this guy. I tried to be mindful when making choices and I veered very carefully away from men who drank frequently and those who could not communicate very well. I became a student of life and processed information carefully." She also learned to identify her needs and wants and to express them clearly.

When she was planning her wedding, she told her dad, "I want you to walk me down the aisle, but you are drinking again. If you are going to drink, I don't want you to come to my wedding." He was angry, but she continued, "Also, I need a check to pay for the wedding—I'm not getting in between you and mom to plan my wedding." She was determined to keep healthy boundaries. After this conversation, her dad went on a binge for a couple months, re-entered the Henry Ford clinic and walked Paolina down the aisle with one month of sobriety. He maintained his sobriety for a year after her wedding.

One Christmas Eve after her parents' divorce, the kids went to her dad's house. Paolina's mom became unglued, screaming and hurling accusations about their lack of concern for her. Paolina calmly took her to another room, removed her audience, and told her very clearly, "This is not appropriate. I want you to get control of yourself and leave." Her mom responded to this boundary and left.

Today, Paolina has very good boundaries with family, co-workers, and friends. She communicates clearly and directly. She conveys wisdom in how she takes responsibility, is accountable, and sets limits. She learned as a teenager how to acknowledge and accept her feelings and speak her mind. Paolina's message is hopeful and inspirational because her mom intervened in the family dysfunction to teach their kids a happier and healthier way to live.

Paolina is not your average parent. She is strong, thoughtful, clear-thinking, and processes information quickly. She is clear on her values and communicates them to her family and friends. She and her husband have a successful marriage and are very close with their kids, spending lots of time together at their colleges and on trips. The family has lots of fun, but it is always under the watchful eye of "mother bear." She directly talks to her kids about choosing their partners wisely and about emotional and chemical health. Also, Paolina knows when it is the time to "let go and let God." The kids know exactly where they stand with their parents and are clear on family expectations.

When I heard Paolina's story, I cried. *Her* mother and father changed the course of their kids' lives by reaching out to a competent resource for help. I can't imagine how helpful that would have been to all of the "big adult kids" I interviewed for this book.

Your mental health is dependent on having clear boundaries with others. There are many things you can do to improve your boundaries, including attending Alanon groups and professional counseling. The following assessment will help you gain clarity on the strength of your boundaries. Ask yourself these questions:

Boundaries Self-Assessment

1. How do you know when one of your boundaries has been crossed (e.g., anger, knots in your stomach, rapid breathing, feeling anxious)?

2. What types of situations make it more difficult for you to maintain your boundaries (e.g., when the other person is angry or crying)?

3. Who are the people in your life who expect you to always be in a caretaker role at the expense of yourself?

4. What phrase can you use easily and quickly when a boundary has been crossed for you?

A term frequently used in psychology to describe one who places a low priority on one's own needs while being excessively preoccupied with the needs of others is codependency. Codependent relationships, where people are not sure where their space stops and another's begins (bad boundaries), are unhealthy. Many of the people I studied struggled to form boundaries as young adults because they grew up in chaotic and enmeshed families bouncing from one crisis to the next.

A key technique to developing your boundaries includes practicing saying "no." Say *no*, with no excuses. Okay, go ahead and smile if you need to do so while saying *no*. Identifying and fortifying your own personal boundaries is a cornerstone to recovery from childhood problems and to becoming an autonomous and fully functioning adult. There will be negative fallout when others realize they can't get you to do what they want like they used to. Interdependent relationships in your personal and work lives, where there is an equal give and take, are the healthy goal. The upsides of having strong and clear boundaries in your personal and work lives are better relationships and a lot less stress for you.

In summary, growing up without clear boundaries at home can result in not having boundaries as an adult. Personal relationships with a spouse, child, or a friend, become confusing and stressed when boundaries are blurred. Work can become cumbersome and professional boundaries blurred when the adults who have weak boundaries at home start doing the same thing at work—taking care of others as a way to take care of themselves. Healthy boundaries establish independence and autonomy from being controlled by other people's problems, feelings and thoughts. Defining and clearly communicating your boundaries will ensure that what is happening around you is safe and healthy for you and is also an expression of your own personal needs and wants.

Chapter 8
Negotiate Conflict Well

Conflict resolution skills are vital for healthy relationships at home and work. However, growing up in a chaotic family where conflict was handled poorly—where people may actually have gotten physically hurt during arguments—can inhibit one from enjoying a good debate.

A serious disagreement brings out the worst in people. The struggle to gain power and win propels some into fight mode, makes others freeze, or flee a situation. Not knowing how to negotiate conflict well harms marriages and relationships with children and friends.

Guess which people in my study and interviews were not comfortable arguing a point to closure? People who had abusive family backgrounds or an alcoholic parent found it challenging to enjoy a good debate at work. They often did not have comfortable and easy-going relationships with co-workers, which make for easier negotiations when problems arise. The individual with an abusive family history may become overly aggressive or too passive.

Managing conflict well is a critical adult skill. The bigger your family or the more responsibility you have at work, the more frequently you will be called upon to engage in conflict negotiation or management of problems. A successful manager must learn to negotiate conflict professionally, keep their perspective, and not take it personally.

What are your default behaviors when tension rises? Be honest with yourself. Anxiety? Anger? Passivity? Drinking? Overeating? Negative self-talk?

If you did not grow up in a family that role-modeled good conflict negotiation skills (and how many of us did?), it is important to learn practical strategies recommended by those who are good at it. Calmly engaging in conflict-ridden situations and influencing and persuading others to see your perspective are critical to being effective at work (and home). Many of those I interviewed consciously studied interpersonal communication and managerial skills to offset the negative interactions they experienced as children. Determining your values around conflict and choosing to practice a specific conflict negotiation model can give you skills to greatly enhance your well-being, thereby creating a less stressful headspace.

How to Manage Conflict Well

Effective and accomplished women and men state they are *comfortable* arguing a point to closure when a difficult situation arises. I asked successful leaders in my study how they learned to communicate assertively and resolve conflict. Their comments about conflict each illustrate an important point about resolving issues well. Read the following quotes from highly successful people to determine which of these behaviors and conflict negotiation styles would best suit your personality and needs.

"My father taught me *conflict negotiation skills.* He loved to argue and would take the other side of an argument to keep me engaged. Women generally do not like to work in an environment of conflict, and I think that is a reason they have not done better in the workplace. Men can have a significant conflict, agree to disagree, and move one. Women tend not to be able to do that."

—Executive Managing Director, International Finance

"From the martial arts. I obtained a black belt in karate. This process forces you to *face your fears* and handle conflict, *without aggression.* It may seem paradoxical, but martial arts are a path of inner peace and complete confidence and calm."

—Consultant, Private Practice

"I have handled conflict by *ensuring decisions are transparent, fair,* and that all impacted are given the appropriate opportunity to provide input. I began learning to communicate effectively in business school."

– President, Healthcare

"I watched a mentor who had a gift in the area of being *assertive*. I *emulate* her every day—I also pay attention to how it feels to interface with an individual who is assertive with *good boundaries*. I try to replicate the technique."

—President & CEO, Marketing

"I value communication. I would *work at the message* I wanted to deliver for hours and days before delivering it. I learned to wait. It was more important that the message be right than rush something out. I also learned to acknowledge differences, rather than gloss over them. Making statements like, 'That is interesting, tell me why you feel that way.' 'Help me understand your position.' Rather than feeling threatened by difference, I found it an opportunity to refine a strategy."

—Managing Partner, Law Firm

"When possible, *don't make the conflict personal.* Let the other person know you are interested in hearing their opinion because once they feel personally attacked, they will lock onto their position even harder. Look for a logical solution that is best for the company and has the best in mind for the greater good."

—VP Operations, Healthcare[23]

These actual comments from well-seasoned leaders illustrate important points about engaging in conflict at work. You may be realizing that you avoid, freeze, flee, or become aggressive when challenged. To begin handling conflict better, learn to develop skills to verbally articulate your concerns, feelings, and needs.

Video and Film Producer

Steve at first appears mild-mannered and laid back, but once you converse with him it is easy to hear his intensity. Steve has been the owner and president of several large video production companies, one of which he took public to great success at age twenty-four. His video production companies won over one hundred national and international awards. Steve has bought and sold fourteen companies and at seventy-three he is starting a new company in a new industry.

He started our conversation humbly by saying, "As a young kid I did not experience a lot of adversity. I am from a small family and had only one younger sister, who pestered me quite frequently. My adversity came in the form of a controlling mother. She was bright and stifled in her career; therefore, her self-esteem came from micromanaging us to ensure we would succeed at everything we tried." Steve's mom told him over and over again that he would succeed at anything and everything—absolutely—he felt tremendous pressure. He said that not only were his mother's career desires curtailed, but she had lost her younger brother, turning her grief into paranoia about her own children. Steve's dad also had an affair for several years and his mom waited for him, which caused great disruption and adversity in the family.

Steve added, "I could never be good enough. I was always doubted and suspected of not doing the right thing. I always got caught. We had tremendous conflict from the time I was ten years old to seventeen, when I left home. I tried to avoid the conflict but was held hostage as a kid. We sparred fiercely and shouted, but I never won because she was the parent and had the power. We both said hateful things and an hour later we would hug and make up. I internalized my mom's focus on performing and doing the right thing. This caused me to become super responsible in life and to take conscientiousness to a fault with my fellow workers and friends."

Steve internalized how his mom treated him and others and now he treats himself in the same manner. He also learned to equate love and work with drama and pain. He did not experience hunger, poverty, or physical abuse, but ongoing verbal and emotional abuse. Interestingly, his mom eventually became a police officer and then a very successful business owner.

I asked Steve how this relentless focus on perfection and achievement affects him as an adult today and he admitted that he has a fear of failure. "Anything less than perfection for me is a failure. I have also been obsessed with reliability and feel incredibly let down when others do not follow through with their commitments. If someone 'drops the ball' I feel overwhelmed with feelings. When I was the owner, producer, and director of a film video business, I needed everyone on location at a specific time because their specific skills were needed to film. These artistic entrepreneurs were freelancers and often would not follow through. I would pull the person aside, explain the cost and schedule consequences of their lateness or absence. I would explain to them that if it happened again, I would have to fire them. I would feel an incredible rush of adrenaline in every part of my body. I would fight against the physiological feelings, and I would try to avoid conflict."

I asked Steve about the specific steps he would follow to handle conflict in light of such a negative past experience with his mom. He explained that he is a member of the Bahá'í faith, which emphasizes individual responsibility to bring about a better, peaceful, and unified society. As a Bahá'í, he says that he respects the views of everyone and tries not to dominate others to fulfill his expectations. Based on his fifty years of business experience and his spiritual values, Steve recommends the following to manage conflict:

- Be aware and admit to yourself that you are angry.
- Pause and consider consciously how to approach the person.
- Reflect on what you specifically want to say.
- Change the goal from expressing anger to having a conversation.
- Provide feedback that is observable.
- Encourage the other person to communicate their views.
- Talk things out until a resolution is reached.

Steve uses this conflict negotiation model, based on his spirituality, in his work life with employees and also with family members.

Joy's Avoidance

Unlike Steve, who developed an effective way to manage conflict, Joy remained stuck in childhood patterns to her own detriment. I interviewed Joy, who has held management and leadership positions, often in male-dominated companies, for the past twenty years. She stated emphatically, "I hate conflict. I am not good at it, and I know it is a problem for me. If something really hurts my feelings, I have a visceral reaction that is overwhelming. It almost goes beyond a fight or flight response to an absolute disappearance into myself and I retreat. Sometimes, if I am angry at someone and hurt, I can disappear for days."

Joy added, "I recently was hurt by something my boyfriend said about his history with other women. Now, on the one hand, I cognitively know what he said was just plain downright stupid and the best way for me to have handled it was to not take it personally and tell him that that was disrespectful. And I tried. But when someone has hurt me deeply, I retreat. I am sure it is confusing to the other person."

Joy stated, "I know as a career woman I should 'embrace conflict' and handle it better, but I am forty-five. At what point do I get to just take care of myself? I was a shy and pretty high school student who lacked assertiveness. I was constantly teased and poked at for a reaction about my appearance, my working-class family, and lack of athletic ability. The other students relentlessly bullied me throughout my high school years. I was miserable. Even the teachers would say mean things about my performance with disregard for how they made me feel. Luckily, I had two good friends to rely on for support who also were gentler in nature. I have also had turmoil in my personal life. As an adult, I am exhausted from having put up with my ex-husband's, father's, sister's, and my own kids' bad teenage behavior. At this point in my life, I want peace and quiet! I surround myself with more caring and gentler people."

Joy continued, "One of the things I am aware of is that after the years and years of verbal and emotional abuse by my father and his abuse of my mother, I probably will never be good at managing conflict. The feelings of anger scare me. I muddled my way through it with people I supervised and co-workers and my kids, but it has never been comfortable. On the flip side, probably as a result of the problems I experienced as a kid, I am very caring and compassionate. I err on the side of giving others too many opportunities to correct their behavior. I did eventually learn to give feedback to my employees well, with kindness and behavioral observations, and encouragement. But, in a relationship, a flaw I have is that I give and tolerate way too much bad behavior, and then I have a tolerance break. When I am done, I am done. And that is the truth about me and conflict. I am not good at it, never will be, and still afraid of the consequences when I disagree or express anger to someone I love. There is just some damage you don't heal from." Some of Joy's difficulty in negotiating conflict may also be due to cultural norms for her sex.

Sex Differences

There may be more differences within a gender than across genders, but Dr. Deborah Tannen, Georgetown professor, has published volumes of research showing that women speak in "rapport" talk, whereas men talk in "report" talk. Rapport talk is focused on feelings and the well-being of others, which may work to your detriment during conflict negotiations.[24] Being overly focused on others' feelings and needs causes you to lose sight of your own goals. Men focus on relaying facts and information, which is conducive to conflict negotiation tactics. Not only does gender-stereotyped communication make conflict more difficult for women, but my research also clearly demonstrated that women were judged more harshly when expressing anger at work. In addition, because so many women have been the object of misuse of power, it may be more difficult for them to “own” their power. I recommend female leaders admit the power differential and consciously decide what kind of communication style they want to embrace. Denying your power confuses everyone. I recommend both men and women combine assertive competence with a supportive stance to influence others at work. Male and female study participants also noted the following workplace communication problems for women specifically:

- Judged more harshly for expressing anger
- Female leaders are expected to communicate like men
- Must communicate in a competent yet friendly manner
- Expected to be better communicators—never too harsh and direct
- Subordinates are less comfortable with and less comfortable taking direction from women
- Penalized for winning

None of the myths about women held true, such as women are more reactive to others, more passive or more emotional, less analytical or care less about winning, or gossip more. Five out of ten women reported having experienced gender prejudice and discrimination that affected their work lives. Ninety-eight percent of the men and women said there were specific obstacles for women in work and financial success. Over 50 percent said they absorb most of the household and childcare duties. These study results point to the concept that conflict management at work may be more difficult for women than men, thereby increasing the need for practice and guidance from supervisors.

Assertiveness

The key to avoiding "over the top" conflict is to *identify* your needs before you feel frustrated and communicate them to the other person. Assertiveness involves *speaking up and asking for what you want*. Identify what is bothering you in any situation and decide how it could be resolved to your satisfaction. Reading about assertiveness will not be very helpful. Becoming more assertive is only accomplished through *practicing new habits*. Start with small issues and then continue onto issues that are more complicated and threatening. Speak up and ask for what you want. Be graciously assertive. Learn to feel big, confident, and in charge. Through practicing new habits, you will become more assertive.

Conflict Negotiation Checklist

As you approach a conflict-ridden situation, review the following checklist to ensure you are approaching the problem in a thoughtful and proactive manner. Preparing yourself internally with the right mindset makes a big difference in the end.

- View conflict as a way to move forward along an agreed-upon path.
- Keep your sense of humor.
- Know the facts and the data well.
- Use your relationship to figure out what the other person wants.
- Know what you want and stand your ground.
- Practice arguing to be comfortable.

- Let emotions subside before taking action.
- Lean into and tolerate the discomfort you feel during conflicts.
- Think strategically beforehand.
- Identify and ask for what you want.
- Don't be overly flexible—adapt, but don't give up.
- Stay optimistic about reaching a solution.
- Give the other person something they want.
- Step back, observe yourself to help tolerate your distress.

Conflict Tips

My study participants also had pithy general recommendations about managing conflict at work. Here are their senior-level recommendations:

- Cultivate a competitive spirit.
- Use quiet determination.
- Know when to break the rules.
- Try new approaches to convince people—use social influence.
- Welcome conflict.
- Practice assertiveness and conflict management techniques.

- Prepare yourself with facts.
- Learn the art of a healthy debate.

Choose a model of conflict negotiation based on your values. Not choosing a model to use for conflict negotiation will result in you falling back into destructive habits you witnessed and formed as a child.

Effectiveness in your personal and work life rely on improving all your communication skills. If you grew up with family members yelling, swearing, and hitting to express feelings and needs, it is a difficult road to become an astute communicator. But, unless you want to stay as frustrated as you may be now, you don't really have any choice but to study, learn, and practice new communication techniques. Expand your repertoire to include humor, compassion, directness, and being succinct.

Each of us has a unique tolerance for conflict and a level of skill for conflict resolution. People who are extroverted and have a low level of neuroticism may naturally have an easier time wading into and sorting out conflict. And people who have grown up in warm but argumentative families are more naturally skilled when arguing their points than others. However, if you have grown up in an abusive family, you may avoid conflict, but you can learn to overcome this hurdle. Many can get past the idea that argumentation is the kind of yelling and emotional drama they experienced in their childhood homes. They choose a model, practice new skills that become habitual, and discover that the rewards and respect from others make it worth the effort.

Chapter 9
Getting Out of An Unhealthy Relationship

The ultimate goal is to have a supportive and happy personal life, while at the same time being successful at work. The most important decision you can make for your overall well-being and career is who you choose for a relationship. Being in an abusive adult relationship at the same time you are trying to be a good parent or succeed at work is like trying to swim to the surface of the ocean after a dive with your feet tied to the bottom. We lie to ourselves and say we can succeed despite the ongoing abuse at home, but it makes the swim much more difficult—for both women and men.

Gabriel

"She was alpha and I was beta," says fifty-year-old Gabriel in a charming and trustworthy sort of way. With a smile that lights up a room, Gabriel states, "Can you tell me the definition of happiness? Because I couldn't find it with that woman after twenty years of marriage." He experienced lots of mind-blowing sex, lots of friends, parties, and trips to Jamaica, Hawaii, New York and California. He adopted her toddler, and they went on to have three more children together. Gabriel stated, "She was beautiful, and we had fantastic sex every day." There was also hitting, screaming and swearing every week. She was taller and twenty pounds heavier than him—and much more aggressive. After years and years of her abuse, he said, sheepishly while looking down at the table, "I hoped it would all end by her getting in a car accident."

I asked Gabriel what the early years of marriage were like. "She chose me," he said. She said, "I think we should get married." And he smiled, shrugged and said, "Okay." His expression conveyed a feeling of—it was up to her, whatever she wanted, no big deal—as if he himself wasn't worth the time to reflect and make a healthy decision for his future.

Gabriel described what went wrong, "She was disappointed in me professionally because I did not make six figures. I worked for thirteen years for a company but did not finish my electrical engineering degree and her expectations were very high. She had her own business in Miami, but we had four kids and she wanted to retire." Her disappointment in him took the form of sarcasm, entitlement and control. If not her way, there was no way. When his wife, Taylor, did not get her way, she would scream, yell, swear and hit him. He frequently would hold her off. When he would lock himself in a room, she would try to break down the door. He said, "It was exhausting, drained my energy, I couldn't focus on work, and I knew one day I would have to leave."

Gabriel went on to describe how the marriage got worse after Hurricane Matthew. Like so many people in Florida, they lost their home and her business. They relocated to Albuquerque, New Mexico, to live with his aunt's family. Without their friends and careers, the marital problems got worse. Gabriel found himself trying to make peace between two alpha females—an impossible task. Once again, he felt powerless, as if he were a child with his parents. Taylor felt excluded from the family and didn't share the same experiences as Gabriel and his aunt. They would sit at the dinner table, share memories and laugh, while Taylor often declined the invitation to join them. Over the months, the tension increased, and Gabriel felt like he was a pawn. He tried not to take sides.

Like many adult children of alcoholics and those who suffered abuse, Gabriel is very trusting and optimistic to a fault. He has a childlike quality and a learned helplessness that makes him appear approachable and easygoing. He turned a blind eye to his wife's bad behavior—even when he caught her in lies about her daily drinking or stealing. She was entitled, grandiose, superior, contemptuous, and angry when people didn't agree with her. Gabriel would try to "keep a bright light on," but two big lies ended the marriage—the first was when she sold their house and used the money to invest in a new business in New Mexico that went 'belly up.' Gabriel found that out from a friend in Miami who had driven by and seen the sold sign on the house.

The second lie that made him finally leave his marriage was when he found out Taylor had been having an affair. He had been in full "caretaker" mode while she was being treated for pneumonia and he brought her computer and iPhone to her in the hospital. There was an ongoing record of her communication with her young boyfriend, even discussing their anniversary celebrations together. Wait a minute—while she was married to Gabriel? Yes. Technology makes it easier to have an affair, but it also makes it easier for the affair to be detected.

I asked Gabriel if he knew how he got into such a bad marriage, other than the superficial things like her beauty and sex. He said, "It might have something to do with having an alcoholic and very verbally abusive dad. My parents divorced when I was twelve years old, and my siblings were away at college. I was there alone and I, along with my mom, was a target. I tried to mediate between the two of them."

I understand now that Gabriel has a "big tolerance for crazy" based on his childhood. He doesn't have a healthy and caring template for intimate relationships. When he talks about his past, there is a learned helplessness, an attitude of acceptance and resistance to changing his life to get better. He was settled in his dysfunctional marriage despite the verbal and physical abuse until he found out about his wife's long-term affair. Letting someone else choose you and then "settling" is a common characteristic of adults who experienced dysfunctional abusive relationships with one or both parents.

I asked Gabriel how this twenty-year abusive marriage affected his self-esteem. "I question others more now and am less trustful, but that is good, right?" He went on to say that he would have finished his electrical engineering degree, but the stress of ending the marriage had been too great. I asked Gabriel if he had advice to others who are in abusive relationships and he said, "Decide how much you are willing to tolerate. I accepted and tolerated a boatload and let it derail my education and career. I plan to put it behind me and not let it affect me professionally any longer."

No one else knows what happens between two people in the hours between dinner time and the next morning when individuals go to work, classes, or take kids to school. However, those interactions have a profound impact on your self-esteem and can increase your well-being, make you more resilient and provide a buffer against the world. Or they can tear you down, make you feel vulnerable and destroy the essence of who you are.

Fran

Fran met her future husband when she was twenty-two years old, after moving to Boston. She grew up in a happy and healthy family and therefore was unfamiliar with domestic violence. She is a lively person and admits she is attracted to powerful people. Fran and her future husband worked together at a Fortune 100 company and dated for one year before she agreed to marry him. She had experienced one abusive incident before their marriage when she described him as her friend, not boyfriend, and he totally became "unwound"—screaming, yelling and acting very intimidating. On the day of her wedding her dad cautioned her, "You don't have to go down the aisle. I want to make sure you know that I am always here for you." Obviously, in retrospect, her father saw something she was not yet aware of. Fran haltingly said, "The honeymoon in Bermuda was awful. I was never good enough for him."

What ensued was a surreal experience of ongoing and frequent domestic violence. On her first day at Harvard for her MBA, she had a black eye that she covered with makeup. Her husband wanted to go to Harvard also and was jealous. They had a beautiful home and two children, but she had left a great job to become a student, and this had increased their financial stress. Her husband was a smart, powerful narcissist. He drove a Porsche, and everyone loved him. Fran said, "It was hilarious how he had people fooled, but to me it wasn't funny—he was five times bigger than me. Every time my light shone brighter, his would diminish. I was easily convinced I was inadequate because I struggled with dyslexia. His abuse made me fearful, anxious, lowered my self-esteem, and diminished my concentration. It really messed up my mind. He would also kick me and push me. Socially I withdrew because I never knew when he would be in a bad mood." She never told anyone about the abuse until eight years later when she told her sister.

The stress of pregnancy and childbirth increased the abuse. At one point Fran was breastfeeding and her husband thought she was doing it inappropriately, so he screamed at her and strangled her while she held the baby. She lived under horrendous fear and at one point when she was pregnant, she had to lock herself in the basement. Another time she left for a week and stayed at a hotel. Fran continued, "And still another time I called the police, and they told me to go to Starbucks while they tried to calm him down. I kept thinking that this cannot be my life! I was in denial." Fran eventually sought individual counseling with someone experienced in domestic violence and left her marriage.

Twenty years later, Fran is now an author and international speaker who motivates others to success. She is the top salesperson for one of the largest skin care companies in the world and a self-made multi-millionaire. She helps women transform their lives from the inside out. When I asked her if she would have accomplished her great achievements if she had stayed in the abusive marriage she exclaimed, "No! For me to thrive and excel I needed freedom to be myself and travel—not jealousy and abuse." Fran tells her inspiring story to women in many countries. She recommends finding a good counselor knowledgeable about domestic violence.

When I asked Fran if anything positive came out of her tumultuous marriage she said, "I discovered how strong I am, and also other women. Whatever you encounter, you can absolutely handle it. You may choose not to do so for a period, but you can handle it. You realize you are strong enough to make things happen even though there is adversity, and you are distracted from your focus. I never had to fight before my marriage to achieve my goals. I learned how to fight for my goals and be tenacious. I try to be transparent and have empathy for other women and I am a better role model."

Gabriel and Fran both came from well-educated and upscale professional family backgrounds—one with familial abuse and one without. This demonstrates that not only adults with a history of familial abuse experience it as an adult. In fact, 25 percent of all couples report at least one incident of abuse during their marriage.

What was similar for Fran and Gabriel is how they both:

- Felt a power imbalance with their spouse
- Felt inferior and intimidated
- Were impressed with their spouse's power, charisma, and prestige
- Committed to grandiose and narcissistic partners
- Ignored and justified the early warning signs that their partner was capable of abuse
- Were distracted and deterred from their professional goals
- Isolated to keep it a secret from friends and coworkers

Both Fran and Gabriel stated that their toxic marriages negatively impacted them professionally, distracting them from career goals. Common symptoms of an abusive relationship as seen at work include:

- Isolating from co-workers—not participating in social conversation and activities
- Distraction and lack of focus
- Anxiety and an exaggerated startle response
- Appearing sad and depressed
- Careless appearance and hygiene
- Expressions of hopelessness and exasperation
- Freezing or fleeing situations where there is conflict

All these symptoms, if experienced on a long-term basis, create depression, a sense of hopelessness, and can limit you from reaching your highest career goals.

How Does This Happen?

No one intends to get into a relationship to be belittled and demeaned or possibly hit and shoved—especially after growing up in a family where one has been abused, watched siblings be abused, or had a parent scream and hit. We often leave that home and try to forget about what happened, only to think about what happened when visiting for a holiday or sleeping in our childhood room.

We go on with our lives and pick partners that on the surface are dissimilar to our abuser. We reason that he is an artist, and my father was a businessman, or she is an attorney and my mother was a stay-at-home mom. However, below the surface there are probably similar characteristics to your childhood abuser.

In addition, dating is oftentimes referred to as a time of "maximum" deception—our best foot forward over and over again. When first dating someone, we are adored and feel better about ourselves and *finally* have the love we missed as a kid. When dating someone new we don't ask enough questions and then listen to the answers. Instead of asking questions like, "Why don't your children want to spend time with you?" And "Why did your second marriage end?" The unhealthier our childhood, the higher our denial is about bad behavior. The adult child is running as fast as he or she can towards filling up that emptiness from childhood. We ignore any warning signs and enter into committed relationships buying homes and building families.

After years together, stress accumulates and there isn't the daily time to spend adoring one another—the responsibilities of life set in. You may start to see another side to your spouse. A derisive comment or an object thrown across the room surprises you because you have such a positive history together. You "blow it off." He or she didn't mean it. It won't happen again. I am just sensitive because of the family dynamics I experienced as a child, but then a month or two later it happens again.

The feelings are familiar. A sick feeling of knowing how wrong this behavior is because you experienced it before in your family of origin. Maybe you even hear the same words of control and criticism and possibly a part of you starts to think, "I am causing this behavior—maybe there is something wrong with me." The joy in your step is quickly replaced by a feeling of slogging through knee-deep mud just to get through the day. There may also be the fear of being alone. You never had the chance to get the love you wanted in the past and now you have to leave without getting it again! It just doesn't seem fair, does it?

Verbal threats, intimidation and abuse are "alive and well" in college-educated, upper middle-class families. The façade of normality—keeping up appearances of groomed lawns, beautiful homes, fancy cars, and smart kids—keeps the person being abused from speaking up. Dr. Susan Weitzman, author of *Not to People Like Us*, states, "I believe that our society's lack of imagery and terminology to describe spousal abuse in its upper socioeconomic echelons has helped reinforce the isolation that many of these women feel." She explains that because their experience does not fit the way the media portrays domestic violence, they "come to perceive that their torment lacks validity—as if it never really happened, or it wasn't all that bad, or it wasn't really abusive. This diminishment, in turn, feeds their ability to compartmentalize the experience—until the mistreatment spirals out of control and reaches wildly dangerous levels that they are no longer able to keep secret or deny."[25]

Dr. Weitzman describes how professional women often think they are too intelligent or successful to be abused and how this professional status or social class makes the victims more isolated. This also applies to men. Professional men and women believe they should have known better and it is embarrassing.

If you are in an abusive relationship and are choosing not to leave, that decision will take an extreme toll on you. First, living with an unpredictable person creates ongoing anxiety. Your system is being flooded with cortisol and other stress hormones. You are physiologically in a flight or fight mode constantly. It takes so much energy to "pretend" in front of the kids and co-workers that everything is okay that you may find yourself often ill and depressed. Once the kids are old enough to observe what is going on, they will start to have their own problems as it is time for them to individuate. "Mom or Dad hasn't left and is being abused." Therefore, the kids believe it must be really bad to be independent and create your own life. What happens is that the children have unexplained anger, anxiety, and depression. The pretense that everything is okay encourages them to deny their own feelings, and they learn to not trust themselves. Many studies demonstrate that kids who witness or experience abuse grow up with a higher rate of cancer, heart disease, and earlier mortality.

Staying in an abusive relationship results in a loss of your own identity—your own "self." Leaving an abusive relationship requires you to face the loss of belonging and love and this is quite a difficult choice, especially if you consider children, your faith, and finances. Why is it so hard to leave? Often the abusive behavior is sporadic, and it takes quite a while to see the pattern because he or she doesn't treat others this way. You think that if you can "just find the key," you can help your spouse see how much he/she is hurting you. The abuse may not happen daily and so during the positive times, the victim may truly forget about what happened and inflate the happy times as a coping mechanism.

If you decide to seek counseling, choose a counselor who has had training in the area of domestic violence. Many therapists are not trained to understand the abuse of power and oppression that can occur in relationships. Author Patricia Evans (*The Verbally Abusive Relationship: How to Recognize It and How to Respond to It*) states, "…therapists trained in family systems view the relationship as if it were a biological system. If one member (part) of the system changes, the other will change. This is neither a useful nor an accurate description of a relationship in which one person seeks to gain and maintain power over the other." Other therapists are educated to look for the pathology in both individuals and may see a couple for months, only looking for answers to their marital problems by looking into their past histories, never seeing the abuse that is currently going on.[26]

Some therapists say that what the client seeks in an adult relationship is what he or she thinks they deserve, but I see this as another indirect way to blame the victim. I propose that individuals who grow up with alcoholism and abuse have never seen a healthy relationship and don't know it exists—they don't recognize what a solid relationship looks like. Additionally, they have a big tolerance for "crazy" and for not being treated well. *We don't choose it, we just don't actively avoid it because it is comfortable and what we know.*

My own research and interviews also demonstrate that the abusive relationship is more common for professional women and men than believed and that it has a strong impact on one's career achievement. Even though you may not tell your friends or co-workers, they can feel your distraction, distance, and the burden you carry throughout your day.

Three Important Facts

First: Domestic abuse will get worse over time because life has stressors, including children, illnesses, financial worries, and work issues. Once a partner starts verbally and physically abusing the other as a way to establish control and dominate with no consequences, it is reinforcing and will happen again.

Second: It is not better for your kids if you stay. While you think you can protect the kids—and maybe you can for a while—in 65 percent of the families where there is domestic abuse there is also child abuse. Also, even if the kids are not a target, they are watching you and they feel your anxiety and fear. Your children are learning what adult relationships will look like by watching you. Marital strife causes them depression, anxiety, ADHD symptoms and possibly substance abuse. You are increasing the chances of your children modeling their adult relationships after yours. Children use their parents as role models, so it is not surprising that youngsters in a violent home learn to deny and ignore reality as they mimic their parents' attitudes. Boys witnessing domestic violence are more likely to externalize their experience and engage in hostile and antisocial behaviors. They may become aggressive and act out. Girls, on the other hand, are more likely to internalize their behavior and become fearful, shy, inhibited and depressed.

Often, the abused spouse will stay because of a pre-nuptial agreement or post-nuptial agreement declaring joint physical custody of the kids if there is a divorce. However, honestly admit to yourself that the children are not going to thrive anyway growing up in the middle of marital chaos. Get a good attorney and figure out through child advocates or other family members how to protect the kids.

Third: It is normal to feel scared and insecure about leaving. Questions and concerns include: What will happen to my children? Will I have enough money to live? How can I be safe? What will he/she say about me in the community? The biggest issue is that by leaving one has to face the sadness and emptiness from the past that has never been resolved. There will be a time of adjustment or a limbo period where you need to just lean in and tolerate the distress of being alone and making a new life. Going to a women's shelter, attending a support group, or seeking a credentialed and experienced therapist can be very helpful. After a few months, you will feel a great amount of relief about being out of the abusive relationship and can put that energy into a greater sense of well-being and a stronger career.

The Abuser

Dr. Weitzman identifies personality characteristics that abusers have in common. I believe this applies to abusers whether they are male or female. Often, the abuser:

- Lacks empathy towards others' feelings and needs
- Feels a huge sense of self-importance and entitlement
- Is preoccupied with success, power, brilliance, beauty
- Requires excessive admiration
- Is interpersonally exploitative
- Expects automatic compliance with his or her expectations
- Rarely apologizes after abuse
- Attacks the others' sexuality or appearance

There are many clinical diagnoses that fit the male or female abuser, such as borderline or narcissistic personality, but these are somewhat irrelevant. It is simply better to ask yourself:

"How do I feel when I am around this person—loved and appreciated or fearful and anxious?"

If you would like to examine how healthy your current relationship is, take the following assessment.

Abusive Relationships Assessment

I feel "less than" when I am around my partner.	Yes/No
My partner often tells me what to do.	Yes/No
My partner criticizes and corrects what I do.	Yes/No
My partner blames and accuses me.	Yes/No
My partner gets angry when I take an action that is not what he/she recommended.	Yes/No
My partner yells, swears, or demeans me to get their way.	Yes/No
My partner throws things, pushes me, or hits me.	Yes/No
My partner uses me as the brunt of jokes.	Yes/No
My partner never apologizes.	Yes/No
My partner is cold and ignores me regularly.	Yes/No

Even a few "yes" answers indicate that you are in an abusive relationship. Healthy relationships don't engage in the negative behaviors listed above.

If you are in an unhealthy relationship, it impacts your mental health. You may often feel anxious and rarely feel calm. It also impacts your work engagement, and career trajectory. It is nearly impossible to feel hopeful and positive about your future when you are being pushed every day to feel "less than".

If you are in an abusive relationship, you probably feel despair, depression, and trapped. Much of your energy goes into "keeping the peace" every day. Your partner's need to have power over you is draining. This sense of being disoriented, confused, and lost follows you to work. No matter what tactics you employ to hide your distress, people may overhear conversations, gossip, or will sense your distraction and sadness. This negatively impacts your relationship.

Until you are out of an emotionally or physically abusive relationship, you will not realize how it impacts your career and, of course, you personally. When one is in an abusive relationship it feels like gridlock. Women and men get stuck in abusive relationships for many reasons, including worries about children or finances. While working at Honeywell as an employee assistance psychologist, I provided counseling to many men and women, some of whom were in abusive relationships. They, too, needed the insight and support to navigate abuse.

We think of abuse as a women's issue, but it is not only women who are victims. In the 2015 phase of my study, 40 percent of the men and women reported either witnessing ongoing domestic violence, were victims themselves, or had an alcoholic or substance-abusing parent during their childhoods. Just as many men as women experienced these life-changing childhood events. The women were more descriptive in telling how it impacted them personally, but the men's stories, while buried more deeply, were just as common. Abuse of men is under-reported and we also underestimate its impact. Male clients reported verbal and physical abuse similar to women and they use all kinds of strategies—healthy and unhealthy—to cope, including alcohol, humor, prescription pills, prayer, meditation, leaving the situation, and trying repeatedly to reason with the other person.

Abuse is an issue of control: holding power over another person. It may be overt or covert and is usually constant. The victim ends up feeling crazy because so often the abuse takes place behind closed doors, and when the victim tries to discuss the abuser's behavior, it is met with adamant denial, which makes the victim question his/her reality. Patricia Evans, author of *The Verbally Abusive Relationship: How to Recognize It and How to Respond*, states, "If you have been verbally abused, you have been told in subtle and not-so-subtle ways that your perception of reality is wrong and that your feelings are wrong. Consequently, you may doubt your own experience and at the same time, not realize that you are doing so."[27] Of course, this undermining of your reality impacts your focus, confidence, and sense of well-being at work.

When you have an adult abusive relationship, work can be an escape. Work can be an excuse to stay away, which alleviates the immediate stress, but the relationships cannot grow because you are using work as an avoidance tactic. You may get strength from work, and it may allow you to bury grief about your relationship, but you see your kids less. The abuse at home can make you lose confidence, distract you, make you anxious and conflicted. You may feel fearful that others will find out and you will lose your respect/dignity.

I am surprised to meet men and women who do not want to understand their experience of abuse. The relationship is over, and they are not interested in how they chose this type of partner and how it impacted their emotional health. That is one way to proceed with life, but a life unexplored, especially in this area, will result in a lack of integration of the experience. It won't be possible to assimilate it and make different choices in the future. The adult abusive relationship will continue to negatively impact you personally and compromise your mental health. If you have been in an abusive relationship, I highly recommend making time to explore the impact it has had on you.

If you are uncertain about how your personal relationship might be affecting your work, take the following self-assessment.

Impact of Abuse

I am regularly preoccupied with the latest argument I had with my spouse.	Yes/No
I have a difficult time concentrating due to problems at home.	Yes/No
Friends tell me I look tired and sad—they ask me if I am okay.	Yes/No
When friends get angry, I find a way to remove myself from the situation instead of staying and resolving the issue.	Yes/No
I hesitate to tell my partner about new friendships.	Yes/No
I am relieved to leave the house everyday to get away from the stress.	Yes/No
I feel fearful about what might happen when I get home.	Yes/No
I can't sleep at night due to the stress in my relationship.	Yes/No
My partner does not want me to socialize with friends.	Yes/No
I am concerned people can see that I have been crying or see marks from abuse on my body.	Yes/No
I lack energy and enthusiasm for my life.	Yes/No

If you answered yes to several of these questions, it indicates that your relationship is negatively impacting your life. The emotional energy it takes for you to cope at home is draining personal resources that could greatly benefit your life in all areas.

There are many ways to begin the process of recovery from abuse, including:

- Individual counseling
- Support groups
- Domestic violence programs
- Reading books and articles about domestic abuse
- Educating yourself about healthy relationships

Even though Gabriel has a big tolerance for "crazy," he is becoming healthier and making progress toward his goals. Remember, he was home with an alcoholic father who was abusive to his mother while his siblings left for college. Hopefully as time passes, Gabriel, like Fran, will rise above his history of abuse, understand his needs and wants, and learn to express them with a new confidence that demands respect in all his relationships.

Leading marriage researchers and educators, John Gottman and Julie Schwartz Gottman in their book *The Love Prescription: 7 Days to More Intimacy, Connection, and Joy* have developed a blueprint to be a happy couple based on their research of thousands of couples. They wisely encourage couples to be aware of their partner's 'bids for connection' and recommend they frequently turn towards their partner, not away. They also warn couples against communicating with the "Four Horsemen," including criticism, contempt, defensiveness, and stonewalling.

The goal is to feel good about yourself and surround yourself with people who demonstrate compassion and respect for you. Do not re-create your dysfunctional childhood family at work or home as an adult. Be aware of childhood behavioral patterns of caretaking, avoidance, or explosive anger. Even having friends who provide mild, yet constant "put-downs" undermines your confidence.

We make excuses and lie to ourselves attempting to believe that we can be energetic, optimistic, and focused in life while being abused at home. This is a myth and is not going to happen. Abuse is the one hundred pounds of weight you are carrying on your shoulders. If you are being mistreated at home, you have less energy, spirit, and resilience to achieve success at work.

The most important decision that you can make for your overall life happiness is whom you choose for a partner at home.

Chapter 10
Adversity and Leadership

Leadership is an opportunity and a challenge to move individuals together to work in a harmonious and satisfying manner. Who you are as a person is most evident when leading others to complete challenging tasks.

What gets in the way? You have your fears and insecurities from childhood that get triggered by those you supervise. Your healthy and not so healthy behaviors get triggered by employees you care too much about and also the ones you dislike. Of course, there are employees you don't enjoy or may actually make you irritated and anxious, and it may have something to do with your past experiences. This chapter is not to teach you a specific model of leadership, but to encourage you to have the strength to see how your past intersects with the present to create the leader you are today.

This concept was never studied before my 2015 phase of research, which showed that one's childhood has a direct impact on one's leadership style. One leader bluntly said, "After the abuse I experienced at home, I clearly saw the gain in not treating people the way I was treated." This became his mantra for his personal and work life.

After twenty-five years of leadership experience, I am convinced that having a strong understanding of my own adversity helped me overcome obstacles in leading others. However, I have coached many leaders who were swearing, yelling, and being derisive towards the people they supervise. They were referred to me by their bosses and often during a session, they would make the connection between their current stressors, dysfunctional childhoods, and behavior they mistakenly thought was appropriate for work.

If a leader had an abusive childhood but is supervising employees who are healthy and optimistic, the work environment may still be one of productivity and positive morale. Then again, if a leader is unaware of how childhood problems formed in him many negative behaviors, managing employees who have had similar adversities can be highly combustible.

One out of every two of your employees arrives to work carrying wounds from past family abuse or alcoholism—some resolved and some not. Ideally, we would like to believe that they leave their personal feelings and issues at the door on the way into work, but it is not possible to artificially separate the two. If you broaden the category of adversity to also include poverty, childhood illness, death of a family member, mental illness, and divorce the number of employees impacted is 60 percent. Interestingly, childhood adversity was not related to a lack of education of their parents. The parents of the group I studied were much more likely to have college degrees than the average population.

When I specifically asked these high-achieving study participants how their problematic childhoods had made life more challenging, they listed the following lifelong effects:

- Anxiety
- Anger

- Depression
- Overeating
- Detachment
- Low self-confidence
- Low self-esteem
- Poor conflict management skills
- Few social skills

When asked the sensitive question about if there were any *positive* qualities that resulted from surviving early childhood problems, the participants stated they were more:

- Independent
- Capable/driven
- Empathic
- Resilient
- Proud of surviving
- Committed to family
- Committed to lead a values-driven life

These negative impacts and adaptive positive qualities of previous hardships influence one's leadership style. Here are some statements from the leaders I studied that illustrate how kids who survived trauma can transform their serious troubles into a recipe for success:

"I have a very strong sensory perception of attitudes and tensions around people. I have very strong drive and determination. I look out for myself and for the people I care about."

"I acknowledge how wrong these events were for a parent. I had knowledge that one day I would be strong enough to stop the actions (physically) and knowledge that abuse would never be passed on to another generation."

"I believe I gained a sensitivity to and empathy for others who were less fortunate and who also experienced difficulties fitting in. I developed a strong work ethic—almost to a fault—as I strived to prove myself. I developed a self-discipline to do my work, be accountable for it, and to take responsibility for my mistakes."

If you wonder if your childhood adversity might be negatively impacting you at work, take the *Childhood Adversity and Work Assessment* in the appendix of this book. Not only will you identify how your work is being impacted, but you will also identify specific behaviors to change.

A manager's job is to help supervised employees resolve daily work problems and achieve goals. Many issues stem from poor communication and a lack of conflict resolution skills. This chapter will give you specific advice on how to help all your employees excel by tapping into their personal resilience to help them become more skilled at job tasks and work relationships.

The following true stories illustrate the impact of childhood on adult leadership styles.

Charlotte's Web

Charlotte, the CEO of a large nonprofit, had not thought about the connection between her childhood problems, coping behaviors, and her adult work style. Her overly accommodating management style towards employee problems brought her organization to a screeching halt.

Charlotte was the CEO of a large counseling center in Minneapolis, Minnesota. This organization had a multi-million-dollar budget, and the CEO position was very stressful. Charlotte was well-recognized in the community as being a leader in social services delivery. She ran into a "perfect storm" and was removed from her position after fifteen years of service. This decision by the board of directors left Charlotte and her constituents in the community stunned.

The messages about her family background and herself had a profound impact on establishing a lack of confidence that later would haunt her as a leader. Every family has generational stories that are passed down and strengthen some characteristics while weakening others. Charlotte's family stories and her childhood coping mechanisms undermined her opportunity to build confidence as a young adult. As a parent, it is critical to emphasize and reinforce the generational family strengths and positive attributes to your children, not just the problems.

Childhood problems often make an individual more resilient and better able to cope with the career detours and failures that are commonly encountered as an adult. I believe childhood adversity can make employees stronger and more successful, but surprisingly Charlotte disagreed. The following is what she had to say.

"Many of my senior staff had difficult backgrounds of abuse and alcoholism. Maybe it is a matter of the severity of their adversity and the long history of it, but none of them became as successful as I hoped they would. I had development plans for each one of them and kept trying to find the right seat on the bus for each one, but the Peter Principle was well at work. Even though they had achieved director or vice president status, their current and past traumas continually interfered with their work. I was overly sympathetic to their personal problems."

As a new CEO (and Missouri "poor" girl) Charlotte was lacking confidence. Her program director, Anne, was knowledgeable, powerful, and arrogant. Together they would discuss and determine the direction of various programs and then the program director would implement them. The program became her legacy, not the CEO's legacy.

Charlotte's lack of confidence lit a fire under the program director. Charlotte had the formal power, but Anne had all of the informal power and they became enmeshed. Charlotte admitted that Anne "opened up so many worlds to me. She built my confidence as a leader and supported me. She did it all."

Eventually, Anne, with a very severe history of childhood abuse, started yelling and interrogating staff when she did not get her way. There became a repeated pattern of yelling and intimidating not only at her peers, but her boss, Charlotte. Her previous protection and help to Charlotte morphed into disrespect and abuse. "My stomach would turn every time she walked by my window, and I ignored my intuitive feelings about her behavior and made excuses for her. I felt threatened myself and knew I had to do something when Anne's peers started being absent and then resigning."

Charlotte looked incredibly sad. "I was so happy when Anne would cancel our meetings," she said. "I was afraid of her." Charlotte was removed from her position due to the workplace dysfunction and staff resignations that she could not control. The board of directors determined that the only way to move forward was to change the leadership of the organization. This must have been a very difficult decision for the board because it potentially jeopardized funding sources. Charlotte hired an experienced executive coach, but by then the dysfunction had gone on too long and there were continuing resignations and terminations.

One year post termination, I asked Charlotte what she had learned about supervising employees who had varying degrees of childhood adversity that ultimately led to bad behavior at work. She had done lots of painful self-examination to lead her to recommend the following:

- Do your own work to become emotionally mature as a leader.
- If you are lacking self-confidence, privately seek the help of a leadership coach.
- Have clear personal boundaries at work.
- Remember your first accountability is to your organization.
- Value people, but never put their individual needs above the organization's goals.
- Be clear on your role as the leader of the organization.
- Know when to say enough is enough and set limits.
- Provide concrete feedback, follow-up with documentation, and don't make excuses for an employee.
- Follow through with consequences if behavior does not improve.
- Don't analyze and make excuses for bad behavior at work.

- If employees choose not to go to counseling to resolve problems, do not buy into their bad behavior.
- Screen and hire well.

Charlotte's lesson was harsh and life altering. It will probably take her many years to fully process and accept the loss of her coveted position. She had no choice but to abruptly develop a less lenient management style in her new position as CEO of another large nonprofit organization.

Many of the men and women I have counseled and coached at Honeywell, UnitedHealth Group, and Phoenix-based companies were way too passive and accommodating or overly critical and demanding. Both leadership styles create problems—employees running rampant, running the show for the whole group, or being rebellious and resistant. Less frequently (and regardless of leadership style), the most difficult situations I have observed as a leadership coach involve leaders who deny the impact that their own childhood and other personal issues have on their supervisory style, and who are supervising an employee who is doing the same thing. It becomes a blame game.

David's Directives

I interviewed David, the chairman of one of the largest companies in the world, about his experiences with people who come from "troubled" backgrounds, or those characterized by what I call significant adversity, and how it might have affected their management styles. Like many of us growing up in the 1950s and 1960s, David talked about having witnessed "abusive" parenting, but said he personally had enjoyed a stable home, love, food, and a good education. His was a very quiet life in small town America with very few extravagances. He said that lives in general back then were different and pretty “basic” for most everyone. It was a comparatively simple time in which expectations were limited, both in terms of parental expectations and their responsibilities, and the needs that defined basic success and happiness were much smaller. The perceived gap between those at the top and bottom didn’t seem all that large.

David started a paper route when he was ten years old and has been working ever since. He says that he works at this stage in his life because he enjoys it and expects continuing accomplishment of himself. He has accomplished great things professionally—more than most people. In business, he has a reputation for being very direct, demanding of himself and to others, arrogant, and sometimes difficult. As the expression goes, he doesn’t “suffer fools” very well. He is the opposite of Charlotte, the passive leader described earlier in the chapter. By contrast, David is highly successful in his career, respected, and perceived as a very strong leader by co-workers and peers. No one messes with him.

He has a controversial reputation, although others frequently ask for his advice about business, their professional lives, and how to handle difficult personal situations. He is generous with his time and resources.

When I asked David to recall key employees who had come from problematic childhoods, he responded, “Just about everyone has had adversity of some sort in their life, as well as kid experiences that left indelible markings; life and personal growth is about getting over these experiences, keeping them in perspective, and learning from them. There are those who do get over their childhoods, and those who don’t. We are all to varying degrees a product of where we have been and what we have experienced—good and bad. ‘Adversity’ is in the eye of the beholder and there are degrees of it, some obvious and some not. It doesn’t matter what kind, just what you choose to do about it. We all have scars that affect us as people and as leaders. The best thing you can tell someone is that you are an adult now, and it is time to get over it, whatever 'it' is. Maturity is about getting over what your parents didn't do right. They all to varying degrees messed some things up and we all experienced things that scarred us. Move on, learn, do your job and do it well! Hanging on to the past and using it as a crutch for failing is an ultimate waste of one's life."

David went on to say, "Holding employees accountable pushes them to focus, learn new skills, overcome obstacles, and help the organization succeed. The pride they will feel in overcoming and experiencing success *will help one get over the past.*" I believe this to be true and is one of the most important points of this book!

I asked the question, "How have your childhood experiences influenced your style and personality, even though you say you don't recall significant adversity in your childhood?"

His response was, "I am a product of it nonetheless, as I think we all are—the personality of my parents (a very strong-willed, driven mother; a stable, kind, hard-working father) from a small southern town environment that emphasized values, education and work ethic. An experience with the death of a friend's brother brought home the shortness and fragility of life and getting over whatever my parents didn't do so well all plays a part in who I am."

So now we have examples of an overly accommodating Charlotte and a demanding David. Both are successful individuals—one in the nonprofit arena, and the other in the international for-profit world.

Take this brief self-assessment to gain a greater understanding of how your current and past stressors affect your leadership style today.

Self-Assessment

1. A leader leads by example—what behaviors and communication style am I modeling for others?
2. What stressors am I bringing into work with me?
3. What negative childhood messages do I still have about myself (e.g., stupid, awkward, difficult, etc.)?
4. What behaviors did I learn to survive my childhood (e.g., taking care of everyone, working 24/7 and never resting, expressing feelings for the whole family, etc.)?
5. What types of employee supervisory issues trigger an emotional response in me because "it is too close to home" (e.g., divorce, angry outbursts, depression, etc.)?
6. What active process do I use to lead others with an open heart and dialogue?

The appendix includes the complete *Childhood Adversity and Work Assessment*.

Authenticity and Compassion

The several phases of research I completed on very high achievers, along with my own 25 years of management experience building operations, leading transitions, handling critical incidents, and employee problems, confirmed the importance of "the three legs of the leadership stool" described in my previous book, *The Millionaire Mystique*. Effective leadership as described by hundreds of senior leaders, including myself, comes down to:

1. The relationship that you have with others built with trust and communication,

2. The relationship that you have with yourself and managing your own emotions,

3. Industry knowledge, operational expertise, and good old-fashioned management skills.

In my chapter on leadership in *The Millionaire Mystique*, I remind leaders that, "It can be awkward initially to be in a leadership position. The title and responsibility may feel like a sweater that doesn't quite fit. To lead with grace requires knowing who you are which allows you to inspire people to help move the organization toward its goals. Leading with grace means that you can project calmness and clarity even if you don't feel it."[28]

In addition, two important attributes for men and women who lead with grace are *authenticity* and *compassion*. These two qualities are especially important for leading employees who have experienced childhood adversity. Authenticity and compassion can help employees with lower self-esteem and confidence bloom into loyal, effective, and successful employees.

I have over twenty-five years' experience with hiring, supervising, and managing employees in nonprofit and for-profit companies. The style that works best in supervising employees is compassionate accountability. Simply put, this includes encouraging open dialogue, reinforcing risks, no shaming, direct communication, no backstabbing, praising, and celebrating successes. Being supportive and expecting that an individual will perform at their highest level within a reasonable amount of time after a problem increases the morale of the whole work group.

As I mentioned before, a leader needs to manage himself or herself first to lead others well. The Cognitive Reflection Test (CRT) created by Drs. Maggie Toplak, Richard West, and Keith Stanovich measures the tendency of a manager to override an automatic negative response to correct for a better response. The higher a leader scores on the CRT, the more the manager is able to engage in thoughtful reflection, a higher level of reasoning, and the ability to seek more positive solutions. To accomplish more proactive and thoughtful responses, a leader needs to understand his or her internal emotional and psychological landscape as a gateway to their own success.[29] Leaders need to have a clear understanding of how their earlier life shaped them as an adult. If a leader bullied others as a child to deal with his inadequacies, he may tend to do so as an adult. If he carried the workload 24/7 without asking for any acknowledgement as a child, he will tend to do so as an adult.

While it is important to acknowledge how your own childhood problems affect your management style and how your employees carry their own negative, unresolved pasts into the workplace, at the same time it is critical to understand that these employees can become some of your best and highest achievers. As a manager, you can capitalize on their heightened sensitivity to all experiences, including positive and negative work experiences.

For years, social science researchers, including Thomas Boyce and Bruce Ellis, have discussed the spectrum of biological sensitivity to one's context. They have identified certain kids as healthy and resilient "dandelion" children who do well wherever they are raised or ultimately work. Ellis and Boyce also have identified what they call "orchid" children who wither if mistreated or ignored, but "bloom spectacularly with greenhouse care."[30]

Your employees who have had difficult childhoods may require more supervision initially, but the rewards can be great for the whole organization as they blossom. The goal is to turn their personal risk into the organization's gain. Employees with troubled pasts just need insightful direction and support to flourish. As an employer, you have the opportunity and more importantly, the obligation to lead and develop individual employees. We underestimate the importance of a significant adult in the workplace and their influence on an individual employee thriving or withering away.

The irony is that troubled employees may in fact, be some of the easiest people to coach to success if you can help them identify and build on their positive qualities and manage their triggers. For instance, an individual who grew up with abuse, but with high intelligence, may be determined to be different and end up with higher self-esteem than others who were also abused. They may be motivated to get more education than other employees, which strongly contributes to their level of achievement and identity. A positive perception of at least one parent or other adults in their family as stable caregivers may also improve their resilience. Recommendations for managing difficult employees are:

1. Know your own personal sensitivities to divorce, expressions of depression, and anger to know how you might be hampered in a clear and compassionate response.

2. Communicate work performance standards, which holds employees accountable and can motivate them to resolve personal issues.

3. Be firm, communicate the facts, and deliver feedback compassionately. Do not let their expressions of anger or sadness change your message.

4. Refer an employee to internal and external counseling resources. You may want to say, "I believe counseling can be helpful and you may want to call our employee assistance services."

What You Can Do as a Leader

Good leadership is an opportunity for you to grow, give, show compassion, and demonstrate your values and skills. Messages you give as a leader can be framed positively even though fraught with stress. Catastrophizing that something is awful creates more stress, anxiety, and depression. Others will follow your lead. They will follow your lead on how to approach a problem, respectful communication, optimism, how to resolve conflict, and in recognizing others' accomplishments.

Clearly knowing your values around the kind of culture you want to grow increases your efficiency and work satisfaction. Do you value honesty and reward it even when there has been a problem? Is it important for you to recognize achievements? Do you value flexibility and teamwork? Is respectful communication at the top of your list? Are backstabbing and gossip not tolerated? Knowing, communicating, and role modeling your values will dictate your work culture.

Your mindset as to how you approach leadership has everything to do with your effectiveness and peace of mind. Dr. Kelly McGonigal, stress researcher, suggests the following to change your mind set about any challenging situation:

"The most effective mindset interventions have three parts: 1) learning the new point of view, 2) doing an exercise that encourages you to adopt and apply the new mindset, and 3) providing an opportunity to share the idea with others."[31]

Take for instance, the situation where two departments are required to merge to accomplish even more difficult operational goals. A leader, unaware of his or her impact, may express discomfort, stress, frustration, and anger. If so, the employees will undoubtedly do the same. However, the leader who pauses and determinedly examines all of the possible positives from this merger will adopt a new mindset. During the staff meeting the leader will have practiced positive and enlightening statements and communicate these to the group, such as: "The work will be redistributed in a more stimulating and challenging manner which will result in growth and opportunities for most of you in this department." In individual meetings with employees to hear their concerns, he will still communicate the same new point of view about new meaningful and important work and the rewards that will follow. Consistently sharing the same ideas with the group over time will change their group mindset into one more accepting of change.

During times of stress people reach out to others in a very primitive fashion looking for comfort. Use this time to develop more cohesion in your team and better working relationships. Creativity is also increased when there is less fear of failure and shame.

A boss can decrease or increase the shame in a group. If you make yourself vulnerable and admit mistakes, your group will have less fear about doing the same. Whether you like it or not, your supervisees will know what time you come into work in the morning, when you go to the restroom, and when you leave. They are highly sensitive to your attitudes and behaviors—they are contagious. This is a great opportunity to humanize work and make it a culture of hardiness. Creating a team that can withstand strict deadlines, mistakes, and problems and bounce back to continue growing and achieving creatively, is a hardiness goal that helps the whole organization.

Your feelings are so often determined by your thoughts about a situation. In difficult situations, it is important to let yourself not be right or wrong but sit with the strong feelings until new ways of knowing and seeing yourself and the world emerge. Approaching employees in an open-hearted manner creates trust and cohesion. Generosity, patience, trust, self-acceptance, and a willingness to share yourself with co-workers greatly enhances work teams.

In my study on factors that lead to success, 99 percent of leaders recommended the *transformational style of leadership* as most effective. Transformational leadership requires a strong understanding of your own strengths and obstacles in relationship building. The specific style includes:

- Communicating a vision
- Empowering employees
- Providing support
- Leading by example
- Seeing each employee as an individual, knowing their strengths and weaknesses, developing a plan for their growth
- Rewarding individuals and work groups for their successes

As bosses, we have employees that we like and others we dislike. We may even be repulsed by some. You can be a successful manager without identifying personal issues that subordinates trigger in you based on your childhood, but your leadership experience will be much easier and rewarding if you know your own internal landscape. Engage in the lifelong process of identifying the employee behaviors that make you anxious. Identify which employees make you feel insecure or threatened, and what situations make you unnecessarily controlling or passive. When is it difficult to set limits with problematic work behavior, and what type of conflict is most difficult for you to handle?

As a supervisor, leader, or boss, you are in an ideal position to be that "other" adult that teaches your employees skills to help them thrive. As a leader you can change people's lives while just doing your job well. Employees who have experienced childhood problems are most of us. Therefore, I want to encourage you to rejoice in your opportunity to help others heal from past wounds and to reach their professional goals. It is straightforward and perhaps will help to heal yourself at the same time. The benefits to employees and the overall workplace are long lasting, significant, and substantial.

Great leaders love new and challenging experiences. If these recommendations seem uncomfortable to you, approach this type of leadership with optimism and enthusiasm, which is probably how you achieved what you have attained thus far.

Good, solid leadership is not about power or prestige—it is about helping others to successfully get the job done. As a leader, know your strengths and weaknesses and be able to identify adversity issues in others. This is a 'must' for leading with grace. Such self-knowledge gives you the calm assurance and indelible footprint that will inspire others to help you move your organization toward its goals.

The workplace obviously has no obligation to help you heal from your past wounds, but it inadvertently has a major impact on how you mature through adulthood. Opportunities to try on new roles, succeed, and be rewarded help heal wounds from the past. A caring and authentic leader with a calm mind more easily coaches employees through minor and major detours. What is your leadership mindset?

Chapter 11
Zoomers and Millennials
Cautionary Tale and Recommendations

New Research

Psychology graduate students, Shannon Burke, Steven Rodriguez, and I were intensely curious as to how the Covid-19 pandemic affected young adults on their journey to achieving satisfying personal and work lives. Many of them entered the workplace when there wasn't even one to go to. Those years were filled by a global health crisis and social unrest influencing their views about life and work. Death touched their lives in an unexpected way. Sixteen percent of respondents had an immediate or extended family member die from Covid-19 and 7 percent had an acquaintance die.

We conducted a descriptive research study, *The Impact of The Pandemic on Young Adults: Adaptive Behaviors and Recommendations*. The results were astounding and illustrative of:

- The impact of the pandemic on their mental health
- Behaviors to avoid during times of extreme stress
- Recommendations on how to thrive personally and professionally
- Workplace recommendations for greater morale and retention

The survey participants were aged twenty-two to thirty-two years old, zoomers (Gen Z) and millennials. Thirty percent were married or living with their partner and 3 percent had children, complicating their Covid experience.

Seventy-one percent of respondents were employed full-time, working in over forty industries. Sixty-three percent worked from home or a combination of home and in the office. They were kept company by their pets—55 percent of them! Before the pandemic fifty percent had been diagnosed by a mental health professional with depression, anxiety, or post-traumatic stress disorder (PTSD.) Essentially half of the respondents had previous mental health concerns and were comfortable seeking access to professional mental health care.[32]

The Impact

The pandemic had a significant impact in worsening their mental health. Ninety-six percent of the participants self-reported frequent feelings of depression or anxiety during the pandemic. Forty percent reported feeling nervous and anxious, 16 percent felt depressed, and 24 percent reported feeling little pleasure or interest in normal activities over half of the days during the pandemic. Seventy-one percent reported excessive worrying and 12 percent said they were worried daily. Clearly the pandemic had a huge impact on the mental health of young adults.

We asked the zoomers and millennials what was the most difficult experience for them during the pandemic. Participants reported a profound sense of isolation, often living alone and being separated from friends and family. When they did see family and friends there was often tension regarding the validity of new information on Covid-19, politics, and social and racial inequality. They reported social media and the news harmed their mental health. Their concern about family and friends was complicated by differing opinions on the issues listed above. Respondents described how societal instability complicated their own fears and uncertainty about the future.

It was indeed a very lonely time for many young adults who were alone in their apartments solely with a pet for company facing illness, death, challenges in new careers, and personal and health insecurity/fears. Many had not been independent and out of their family homes for long creating further emotional and financial insecurity.

Individuals working in healthcare witnessed an extreme amount of death, oftentimes without the correct protective gear and management uncertain and unable to best support their employees. Many reported an unsupportive work environment further negatively impacted their mental health.

I provided counseling to clients in their twenties throughout the pandemic. They worked in healthcare, lived alone in new cities, often witnessing death on a daily basis, and had profound fear and sadness. Developmentally, it was a punch in the gut to be on their own without family support during a societal crisis.

One participant stated: "January 2021–June 2021 was one of the most difficult periods. I had a lot of feelings of helplessness, hopelessness, and hated where I was at in life and what I was doing. I went multiple days without sleep due to stress and felt like I couldn't do anything right. It got to the point where I wasn't sure how I was going to make it to summer break. I hadn't planned anything related to suicide, but I was numb and depressed and not sure how I was going to get through it."

And, some that were married (14 percent) also had concerns and said: "Trying to live with my husband while he was abusing me and not having another place to go was incredibly challenging. Now living with new roommates that I don't know well and trying to get a divorce is a new challenge."

And another participant reported, "My wife and I disagreed on how much exposure we wanted to have due to my elderly and ill parents. We were both afraid but had different opinions on when and where to go out, whether to wear masks, and the safety of new vaccines."

Negative Coping Behaviors

During times of hardship, it is difficult to tolerate emotions. It is painful and there is a tendency to numb ourselves with food, alcohol, drugs, or sex to try to escape feelings, however this does not build the "muscle" for new behaviors to increase resilience. Bad habits that provide quick dopamine "hits" are not a long term solution to deeper issues. Previous research illuminates individuals' poor coping strategies can result in long term problems. This group of zoomers and millenials reported they engaged in the following negative coping behaviors during the pandemic :

- Internet use/social media (81%)
- Alcohol use (80%)
- Isolating (52%)
- Excessive sleeping (46%)
- Overeating (35%)
- Recreational drugs (30%)
- Gambling (5%)

The results of the unhealthy coping behaviors became obvious due to the eventual physical, emotional, and mental health consequences. These consequences prompted them to later make healthier choices.

What Helped Them Thrive

The primary purpose of this descriptive study was to better understand the impact of the pandemic on younger adults and learn from them as to what helped them thrive under stress. It was their opportunity to tell us what helped them personally and professionally.

The helpful habits recommended by the zoomers and millennials included:

- Family and friends
- Pets
- Exercise
- New hobbies
- Journaling
- Meditation
- Partners

We asked what *advice* they had for others their age to thrive personally and professionally during times of adversity. Would it be similar or different to my previous *Adversity and Success* research—what their parents or grandparents recommended in overcoming adversity?

Zoomers and millennials recommendations to thrive personally under duress were similar to what is recommended by wellness experts and reported by boomers in my previous research.

In order of frequency their recommendations are:

- Maintain good relationships with family and friends.

- Be assertive and advocate for yourself.
- Invest time in therapy and have good healthcare.
- Practice mindfulness and/or meditation techniques to manage stress.
- Focus on yourself and find goals and activities that make you happy.
- Become more resilient in any way that works for you.
- Exercise.
- Minimize social media, including the news.
- Create a regular sleep schedule.
- Minimize alcohol and drug consumption.

Professionally, zoomers and millennials recommended:

- Maintain strong boundaries at work and take time off when needed.
- Invest in organizations with healthy work environments and coworkers you can trust.
- Work remotely and have flexibility when possible.
- Have a good work-life balance.
- Seek meaningful work.

Some very insightful and descriptive comments were:

> "Have a life outside of work. Take note of what actually genuinely makes you happy and find more ways to do those things in your life. Value and work towards your own happiness and self-fulfillment like it's your job, because no one else will do it for you."
>
> "Manage what you can control actively, and through self-work and therapy learn strategies to cope with what you cannot externally control. Find your strengths and passions and grant yourself them willingly."
>
> "Don't give up and ask for help if you need it! You won't know how others will respond if you don't ask, and people will surprise you (in a good way!). Also, give other people grace, because you have no idea what they're going through."
>
> "Maximize your learning through experiential or virtual opportunities which immediately increase your knowledge and potential to grow. Ask for more of what you need, whether a raise, a break, a new opportunity, a leadership opening or support. Say no if it doesn't serve you well. It's never too late to go back to school."
>
> "Connect with yourself. What do you love? What do you love about you? What values do you share with others and are those values you uphold well?"
>
> "Learn to be able to live with yourself. Find people you connect with and if all else fails, get a cat!"[33]

How The Pandemic Changed the Definition of Good Leadership

How does a workforce who has lived through a pandemic change what is seen as a good leader? Hands down, a democratic type of leadership was recommended by the young adults who weathered the pandemic—not autocratic, nor laissez-faire.

In one of my past studies, *The Impact of Traumatic Events And Organizational Response*, I focused on bank robberies throughout the country and the impact on direct line staff and managers. Leaders in these organizations experienced twice the number of robberies and were in the difficult position of supporting their employees, while being held accountable to the company's mandates, and at the same time concerned about their own health and safety. The managers reported a significant impact on their own mental and physical health and their own productivity suffered due to their dual role.

I believe this is very similar to what supervisors and managers experienced during the pandemic. The pandemic was difficult for direct line employees, whether working in healthcare or technology, however it was challenging for managers also. How best to lead when you have your own current trauma, organizational financial stressors, and your employees are in great distress?

Employees also bring their current problems with spouses, children, finances, and substance abuse into work. Our most recent research, *The Impact of the Pandemic on Young Adults: Adaptive Behaviors and Recommendations* resulted in data describing how young adults' views about work have changed due to living through the pandemic. They stated that there were actions their employers did well, which were helpful for them to thrive during adversity, and they had very specific ideas on what their employers could have done to better help them.

What Employers Could Have Done Better

- Provide more support to remote workers to combat isolation.
- Make authentic connections with new employees.
- Create ways for employees to get to know one another, inspite of remote work.
- Consider each employee's situation and be flexibile about working from home.
- Ensure employees follow health and safety protocols.
- Be aware of the mental health of your employees.
- Increase our knowledge about human resources and benefits, such as the employee assistance program.
- Give the choice about vaccinations.
- Ensure adequate staffing to decrease burn-out.
- Support boundaries even if employees are working from home.
- Convey leadership understanding and flexibility.

The following real life example describes the degree of stress on a young nurse:

"I worked in a metropolitan hospital and in two years every patient I had died, except one. We didn't have the correct protective gear, were asked to do procedures we weren't trained to do, and I eventually got Covid myself before vaccinations were available. I'm trying to recover from that experience and now my mom just died."

The impact on this young twenty-six-year-old just finding her way in the world of work was phenomenal, increasing her anxiety, depression, and perpetuating a worldview of danger. She has since resigned from this hospital and now works in a setting that she says is much more supportive of their employees.

Previous research on millennials has demonstrated as a group they have different expectations of their supervisors and organizations in general. These expectations were intensified during the pandemic. They expect leaders to build relationships, be respectful, trust, and to speak honestly and clearly. They want their leaders to be authentic, which requires self-confidence, self-awareness, and compassion.

The leader in the twenty-first century authentically needs to build respectful and trusting relationships. The person I know that embodies the type of leadership that is described by the zoomers and millennials is Henry. He is authentic, funny, and has a great amount of self-awareness. He is also transparent. He is co-owner of a business he and his wife built together which now has two hundred employees after just ten years and their business model is robust.

Their employees love working for them. I asked Henry, "How do you manage your employees?" And he responded, "We are an employee centered company. We seek the best workers and put great effort into retaining them. We communicate honestly and authentically. We also show them we value them every day. We have recognition events, celebrate little and big wins, and provide them with the training and support they need to do their jobs."

Henry has a democratic style of leadership, and he sees each employee as an individual. He encourages participation, engagement, and has integrity. This builds a cohesive culture. Both partners have provided an inspiring vision for the future to their employees. His humor may be a bit corny, but everyone is laughing.

We know from my past research, *Pathways to Career and Leadership Success,* that the most desired leadership qualities are:

- Self-awareness to manage your own emotions
- Respectful and honest relationships
- Vision to influence and persuade
- Communication with humility and compassion
- Learning agility and enthusiasm
- Collaboration
- Integrity and authenticity
- Conscientiousness
- Openness to new experiences
- Persistence and tenacity
- Ability to contain worry and rumination

Henry and his business partner and spouse, Connie, embody these traits. They have a high degree of self-awareness and manage their emotions to create a cohesive culture. They effectively inspire, delegate, and communicate well.

Turning Points

Each person I studied and interviewed for this book, regardless of their generation, had a turning point where their difficult circumstances—Covid-19 pandemic, eating disorder, drinking, panic attacks, work problems, or marital problems were overwhelming their lives. In addition, we try to mold ourselves into jobs that harm our mental health, relationships that aren't a good fit, live in cities with polluted air, and strive for achievements to numb us from our pain. Each one came to the realization that without exploration and the courage and discipline to try new behaviors they would not overcome their challenges. Mindfulness of how current or past issues were sabotaging their adult life required discipline and effort. It takes work to change negative self-thoughts and bad behaviors. They were anxious, depressed, and realized their trajectories were only going to get worse. During the pandemic which spanned three years, many individuals tried unhealthy behaviors and alternately made healthier choices as the pandemic wore on. It is possible and probable that the experience of the pandemic as a young adult, fortified this group to make them more tenacious and resilient for the future.

Resilience

Adversity damages your core sense of self-worth, disrupts your lifelong stress response, and negatively impacts your immune system. Resilience through integration is the goal in recovery. The more you are able to withstand negative situations in your life, build new habits, and achieve some successes, you will retain your stability and bounce back to normal after a stressor. Resilience experts, Drs. Steven Southwick and Dennis Charney, believe there is not one specific prescription that works for everyone; therefore, you need to find resilience building skills that work for you as an individual. ***The recommendations regardless of generation point towards the same actions:***

- Develop a core set of values.
- Find the meaning in your adversity.
- Utilize cognitive behavioral strategies and exercises to calm your mind.
- Regulate your emotions through meditation.
- Face your fears and develop self-compassion.
- Understand that all parts of yourself have served a purpose in life.
- Reframe stressful events as an opportunity to grow.
- Maintain a positive outlook.
- Emulate other resilient people.
- Accept challenges.
- Use your support system.
- Learn new things often.
- Find exercise you will do regularly.
- Don't dwell on the past.
- Recognize what makes you strong.[34]

Resilience is not only a mindset but requires *practiced behaviors* that build new muscles to help you survive and thrive during hard times. The following list of activities, recommended by over four hundred research participants from young adults to the elderly, spanning several generations, can help you rebound from setbacks. Developing these habits can help improve your headspace.

- Identify self-limiting beliefs and create more positive narratives.
- Pursue healthy friendships.
- Engage daily in pleasurable activities.
- Set boundaries and learn to say no.
- Achieve work successes.
- Develop a career choice that fits with your values.
- Work for success in love relationships.
- Allow your "God given" talents to emerge—athleticism, intelligence, charm.
- Practice mindfulness and meditation.
- Practice positive self-talk and manage the chatter.
- Seek counseling.
- Enjoy a pet.
- Get out of bad relationships.
- Practice daily self-care—exercise, sleep, good nutrition.
- Spend time in nature.

- Rewrite your story—identify the positives you received from your family of origin.
- Avoid maladaptive behaviors—bingeing, drinking, drugs.
- Identify when you feel helpless and take action.
- Practice gratefulness.
- Attend therapy.

The negative impact of adversity originates in our childhood experiences, however so do the coping skills. I asked a Minnesota-based psychologist and licensed marriage and family therapist, Cindy, to explain the impact on a child when experiencing trauma and how therapy may help an adult later become more resilient. Her thirty-five years of experience inform this comment,

"A child is very vulnerable to messages from their parents and so negative messages become very deeply embedded into their psyche. Adversity affects their thought processes and emotions and damages their core sense of self and worthiness. At the very time when children are learning how to bond or attach with others, there is uncertainty and abandonment, which compromises their resilience. Counseling can be very valuable in changing these patterns to strengthen one for their adult lives, however, it is critical to ensure the therapist you are choosing has the appropriate credentials and experience to be helpful. Find a sensitive and caring therapist to provide witness to your family history."

Today, most therapeutic programs understand the role of childhood adversity and how it results in adult diagnoses of depression, anxiety, substance abuse, or PTSD. It is a given that childhood hardships compromise one's natural ability to be resilient as an adult.

Survivor workshops, such as those offered by the Meadows Retreat Center, have structured week-long workshops to pointedly address childhood trauma and the road to healing. The goal is to identify and release painful emotions from childhood while focusing on self-compassion and creating a healthy life. Because trauma affects our physiology, mind, emotions, and bodies we need a multi-faceted approach to become calmer and healthier as an adult.

Specific techniques within therapy, but which can also be practiced individually, are:

- Assess how your current circumstances, whether a relationship or job, may be helping or hurting your mental health. You cannot overestimate the impact of a 'bad fit' on your mental and physical health.

- Learn how to soothe your mind and body via mindfulness techniques.

- Tell your childhood or adult story to a trusted person to give witness to what happened to you.

- Use cognitive behavioral therapy and dialectical behavioral therapy workbooks to reframe your experiences and learn new behaviors.

- EMDR (eye movement desensitization and reprocessing) allows for a client to access their trauma while in a meditative state and cognitively introduce or interweave more uplifting and positive solutions. This has actually been shown to change brain chemistry and emotional resolution. EMDR helps the client safely experience difficult experiences and focus on their strengths to create an alternative and more positive story. EMDR helps change negative beliefs that are self-blaming into more optimistic thoughts and detach from past fears.

- Literally, rewrite your story to emphasize the strengths and skills you achieved as a survivor. This can be very helpful in focusing away from the trauma and embracing a more positive script for the future. Just replaying the victimization over and over again in your head works to strengthen the negative emotions instead of moving you forward. Writing your story of strength and survival will help you move into today without dragging so much of the past with you.

- Bibliotherapy and podcasts can be very helpful to the recovery process.

Practicing new behaviors diligently every day can help you develop more life skills that eventually become habitual. These new habits, whether cognitive techniques or behavioral changes can calm your headspace.

In addition to therapy, support groups can be helpful, such as Adult Children of Alcoholics, Alanon, Alcoholics Anonymous, or domestic violence prevention programs. (Be aware that some self-help groups are more effective than others, therefore shop around until you find one that works for you.)

Whatever new behaviors you choose to cultivate need to eventually be enjoyable. The positive feelings from your new support group or writing in your journal are what makes the new habits last. Time definitely heals, but the degree to which you heal depends on whether you expend meaningful effort to understand and change your behaviors. James Clear, an expert on behavioral change, described in his book *Atomic Habits*, "Here is how the math works: if you can get 1 percent better each day for one year, you'll end up thirty-seven times better by the time you're done. Conversely, if you get 1 percent worse each day for one year, you'll decline nearly down to zero. What starts as a small win or minor setback accumulates into something much more."[35]

We need to radically acknowledge and accept the past to move into the future. We are not just our past histories and by fully absorbing ourselves in the moment we move forward.

So, you can seek counseling, go to workshops, read self-help books, practice exercises and meditation—or you can continue to have your childhood provide the negative fuel that drives you every day while it appears to be buried. However, peace and happiness won't be as easy to obtain without honesty and exploration of the adversity you have experienced.

This requires setting aside time to reflect, journal, and study to identify and practice new behaviors. It is important to build systems, such as keeping a journal and pen on your night stand , practicing setting boundaries, or attending therapy sessions to improve your insights into how your past experiences are affecting you today. Even small positive changes in your daily habits compound to create a better outcome in the future.

James Clear emphasizes it is important to have a system to improve in any area. He states, "Whenever you're looking to improve, you can rotate through the Four Laws of Behavior Change until you find the next bottleneck. *Make it obvious. Make it attractive. Make it easy. Make it satisfying.* Round and round. Always looking for the next way to get 1 percent better." Overcoming adversity is a process with setbacks AND success is achieved with small steps moving forward. "[36]

Zoomers to boomers have clearly described behaviors and mental health techniques that have helped their well-being and calmed their headspace. Will you try their self-care recommendations and live in this manner?

Recovery requires doing your own work for improvement. The scars of your adversity may never go away, but you can change unhealthy behaviors and create more positive habits starting with small achievable steps today. How do you know if you are making progress? More time for joy, healthier relationships, calmer headspace, and hope for the future. Creating new habits for a calmer headspace creates a lighter and brighter future for you.

Appendix: The Journey

The Journey below summarizes the impact of adversity on one's physical and mental health, resultant personal and work issues, and skills and resources needed to recover.

CHILDHOOD HARDSHIPS

- Poverty • Child abuse • Domestic violence
- Alcoholism • Divorce • Mood disorders
- Illness/death of a family member

IMPACT OF CHILDHOOD STRESS

- Chronic physiological response
- Immune system compromised
- "Fight, flight, or freeze" reaction
- Anxiety/depression
- Shame
- Distracted and inattentive

- Diminished self-esteem
- Low self-confidence

ADULT PROBLEMS

- Poor communication
- Eating disorders
- Alcoholism
- Drug abuse
- Social isolation
- Conflicts at school/work
- Hypervigilance
- Relationship/attachment difficulties

PERSONAL & WORK ISSUES

- Clarity of communication
- Assertiveness
- Conflict management
- Lack of authentic self
- Uncomfortable with power/authority
- Lack of promotions

- Unable to build social capital
- Anxious/avoidant attachment

PERSONAL & WORK SUCCESSES

- Meaningful work
- Challenging positions/assignments
- Healthy relationships
- Assertiveness
- Social influence skills
- Self-confidence
- Positive family dynamics
- Conflict management skills
- Parenting skills

RESOURCES

- Competent counselor
- Support group
- Educational seminars
- Spiritual practice
- Podcasts

- Bibliotherapy
- One supportive, reliable adult
- Mentors
- Employee Assistance Programs

SKILLS NEEDED TO RECOVER

- Discover meaning in your life
- Know your values
- Spirituality/mindfulness
- Choose and practice positive thoughts
- Replace negative thoughts
- Assertive communication
- Exercise, sleep, and good nutrition
- Network of healthy friends
- Conflict negotiation
- Find a good job fit
- Flexibility/resiliency
- Know what makes you happy
- Excel at work
- Practice gratitude

Childhood Adversity and Work Assessment

Key factors that lead to well-being and success at work are: conscientiousness, authenticity, engagement, social influence, openness to new experiences, ability to regulate emotions, being comfortable negotiating conflict, and a minimum amount of worry.

What makes this difficult is that our childhood experiences are carried with us into our adult personal and work lives. One out of every three employees has experienced childhood trauma. This childhood trauma gets triggered at work resulting in self-doubt and overwhelming emotions.

The key to moving beyond being activated by your childhood experiences is to recognize that there are internal and external triggers that may be unconscious. To increase your conscious awareness: identify when you are getting triggered, determine ways to control your emotional hijacking, and have actionable steps that move you towards more thoughtful and mature behaviors.

If you question whether your previous experiences may be negatively impacting your well-being and progress at work, complete the following assessment.

IDENTIFY EMOTIONAL TRIGGERS

1. I have difficulty and feel "triggered" by the following situations at work:

   Arguments or conflict

   Irritability

Crying

Swearing

Competition

Bullying behavior

Being alone with the opposite sex

Touching

Co-workers with personal problems-boundaries

Narcissistic behavior

Overwork or deadlines

Performing in public

Fatigue or illness

Authority figures

Negative feedback

Disciplinary action

Social situations

2. Once you identify that you are being emotionally triggered at work, begin to gain mastery over your emotional reactions by doing the following:

    A. Observe yourself. Notice how you feel when you are around certain people and in various situations.

B. Identify the people and situations that trigger strong emotions and accept that these automatic responses are a part of who you are.

C. Reflect on the origin of your automatic responses and have compassion for yourself.

D. Become aware of your automatic and undermining self-doubts—your negative thinking; change your internal script to a more positive internal dialogue.

E. See this stressful event or person as an opportunity to force development of undeveloped personality traits, communication, or organizational skills.

F. Seek out opportunities to try out new, sometimes opposite, behaviors. Observe and emulate others to determine which new behaviors are the best fit for your personality and work style.

BUILD CONFIDENCE

1. Write down situations or skills where you feel confident.

2. What people or situations make you feel less confident?

3. How do you know when one of your boundaries has been crossed (e.g. anger, knots in your stomach, rapid breathing, or feeling anxious)? Do you have the skills to manage boundary violations?

4. What are the thoughts and feelings that arise in challenging situations?

5. What are the negative messages you received as a child that you have internalized?

6. Implement the following steps to improve your confidence level:

    A. Know your areas of strengths and weaknesses.
    B. Identify the people or situations that undermine your self-worth.
    C. Practice new behaviors to expand your repertoire, such as conflict management skills and assertive communication.

D. Identify and ask for what you want; do not be overly flexible.

E. Lean into and learn to tolerate discomfort.

F. Take care of yourself physically with nutrition, sleep, meditation, and exercise.

G. Understand the "secondary rewards" that may be pulling you towards behaviors that are unhealthy for you.

H. Recognize and replace self-defeating behaviors and thoughts.

I. Develop the habit of self-affirming and positive thoughts.

J. Practice love and compassion for yourself in spite of not being perfect.

INCREASE YOUR RESILIENCE

1. I am aware of and limit my exposure to people and situations that erode my self- esteem.

   Yes No

2. I nurture and am committed to a network of caring and supportive friends and family.

   Yes No

3. I have individuals at work I can confide in and trust.

   Yes No

4. I can experience difficult situations and observe my emotions without over-reacting.

   Yes No

5. I take care of my health through eating a nutritious diet, engaging in physical exercise, and having a good sleep schedule.

   Yes No

6. I regulate my use of prescription medications, alcohol, and excessive eating.

   Yes No

7. I allow myself to see the humor in life.

   Yes No

8. I have identified my values and my life is a reflection of those values.

   Yes No

9. I believe I have control and the ability to act and create a life of my choice.

   Yes No

10. When facing obstacles or failures, I accept responsibility for my actions as a first step to moving beyond the problem.

    Yes No

11. I am excited by challenges that lead me to grow personally and professionally.

    Yes No

12. I am optimistic and feel hopeful about my future.

    Yes No

13. I am aware of and seek activities that nourish and renew me even during times of stress and transition.

    Yes No

Write down three action steps you are willing to start to increase your resilience.

1.

2.

3.

Is your resiliency at serious risk?

Some childhood adversity, if overcome at an early age, may put you on a trajectory toward success, but too many adverse events requires daily attention for you to optimistically problem solve and succeed. *Answer the following questions to determine your level of resiliency risk.*

1. I have experienced more than two adverse childhood events, such as an alcoholic parent, emotional/physical abuse, abandonment, or death of a family member.

   Yes No

2. I would label my childhood as often chaotic.

   Yes No

3. I have been diagnosed with mental health issues, such as depression, anxiety, ADD, or a personality disorder.

   Yes No

4. I have been diagnosed with an addiction.

   Yes No

5. If diagnosed with a physical or mental health issue, I sometimes don't follow through with treatment for my diagnosis.

   Yes No

Experiencing a couple of childhood problems is the national norm and may increase your strength in handling difficulties as an adult. However, too much childhood adversity may result in less resilience as an adult. Excessive childhood adversity requires a very structured plan that you actively work on a daily basis to increase your resilience as an adult.

AVENUES TO RECOVERY FROM CHILDHOOD TRAUMA

- Employee assistance programs—capitalize on a "turning point"
- Individual therapy with an appropriately trained and certified counselor

- Support groups, workshops, and EMDR
- *Meditation practice* to foster self-compassion and emotional regulation
- Lead a values-based life to build your resilience
- Learn to communicate clearly and assertively
- Set healthy boundaries

Acknowledgements

I know many creative and successful people who experienced all types of adversity as a child or an adult. They persevered and went on to create happy and successful lives. The resilience described during our interviews and in all phases of my research was the impetus for this book.

I am very grateful that over four hundred men and women completed my lengthy research surveys and over twenty-five people were interviewed for this book. The stories they shared are poignant, deeply felt, and their recommendations for recovery are specific and realistic. They can change your life!

I wanted to contribute what I have learned about overcoming adversity by creating a clear roadmap, *The Journey Chart*, that will provide guidance in understanding and integrating your experiences to thrive.

Thank you to Dr. Mark Attridge, social science researcher, for his extensive research guidance. Second, I want to thank Shannon Burke and Steven Rodriguez in helping design and implement the 2021 phase of research, *The Impact of the Pandemic on Young Adults: Adaptive Behaviors and Recommendations.*

Third, I want to thank Pat St. Claire, St. Claire Design Studios, for her life long friendship, support, consultation, and design. Fourth, thank you to Wisdom Editions for believing in this project.

Thank you!

About the Author

Jude Miller Burke, Ph.D., is a therapist, business coach, and parent. She spent a decade at Honeywell in Minneapolis providing employee counseling and management consulting. She was a domestic violence therapist for five years at Human Services of Washington County, MN, and has provided leadership assessments and executive coaching at the University of St. Thomas Business Center, Murro Partners, and JAMB Consulting. Dr. Miller Burke is former Vice President of Operations, Optum, at UnitedHealth Group. She is currently a senior consultant providing counseling for a national employee assistance organization specializing in helping those working in healthcare. She also has a private practice in Phoenix, AZ and Minneapolis, MN. She has worked for many years in the Phoenix community as a member of the board of directors for Fresh Start Women's Resource Center.

Endnotes

1 Burke, Jude Miller, *The Millionaire Mystique: How Working Women Become Wealthy & You Can, Too!* (Boston & London: Nicholas Brealey, 2014), 18–21.

2 Burke, Jude Miller, and Attridge, Mark, "Pathways to Career and Leadership Success: Part 1 – A Psychosocial Profile of $100k Professionals," *Journal of Workplace Behavioral Health* 26 (2011): 175–206. Phases 1 and 2 of the study were published in this journal. Phases 3 and 4 are currently unpublished. See also, Jude Miller Burke and Attridge, Mark "Pathways to Career and Leadership Success, Part 2: Striking Gender Similarities Among $100k Professionals," *Journal of Workplace Behavioral Health* 26:207–239.

3 Harris, Nadine Burke, *How Childhood Trauma Affects Health Across a Lifetime,* TEDMED, September 2014, https://www.ted.com/talks/nadine_burke_harris_how_childhood_trauma_affects_health_across_a_lifetime.

4 McGonigal, Kelly, *The Upside of Stress: Why Stress Is Good For You and How to Get Good At It* (New York: Penguin Random House, 2015), xvii.

5 Roberts, Geoffrey, Tone, J. B., & Lieberman M.D., *Feelings Wheel* (University of Central Arkansas, 2018).

6 Quenk, Naomi, *Beside Ourselves: Our Hidden Personality in Everyday Life* (Palo Alto, CA: Davies-Black Publishing, 1993), 234.

7 Gladwell, Malcolm, *David and Goliath: Underdogs, Misfits, and the Art of Battling Giants* (New York: Little, Brown and Company, 2013), 268.

8 McGonigal, Kelly, *The Upside of Stress: Why Stress Is Good For You and How to Get Good At It* (New York: Penguin Random House, 2015), 132–133.

9 Felitti, V. J., Anda, R. F., D. Nordenberg, D., Williamson, D. F., Spitz, A. M., Edwards, V., Koss, M. P., and Marks, J. S., "Relationship of childhood abuse and household dysfunction to many of the leading causes of death in adults: The adverse childhood experiences (ACE) study," *American Journal of Preventive Medicine* 14, no. 4 (1998): 245–258.

10 Felitti, V. J., and Anda, R. F., "The relationship of adverse childhood experiences to adult health, well-being, social function, and healthcare," in *The hidden epidemic: The impact of early life trauma on health and disease*, eds. R. A. Lanius, E. Vermetten, and C. Pain (Cambridge, England: Cambridge University Press, 2008).

11 McGonigal, Kelly, *The Upside of Stress: Why Stress Is Good for You and How to Get Good At It* (New York: Penguin Random House, 2015) 9.

12 Harris, Nadine Burke, *How Childhood Trauma Affects Health Across a Lifetime,* TEDMED, September 2014, www.ted.com/nadine_burke_harris.

13 Madi, S. R., "The Story of Hardiness: Twenty Years of Theorizing, Research, and Practice," *Consulting Psychology Journal* 54, no. 3 (2002): 165–183.

14 Felitti, V. J., Anda, R. F., D. Nordenberg, D., Williamson, D. F., Spitz, A. M., Edwards, V., Koss, M. P., and Marks, J. S., "Relationship of childhood abuse and household dysfunction to many of the leading causes of death in adults: The adverse childhood experiences (ACE) study." *American Journal of Preventive Medicine* 14, no. 4 (1998): 245–258.

15 Brown, Brené, *The Gifts of Imperfection: Let Go of Who You Think You Should Be and Embrace Who You Are* (Center City, Minnesota: Hazelden Publishing, 2010), 44.

16 Klein, Stefan, *The Science of Happiness: How Our Brains Make Us Happy – and What We Can Do to Get Happier* (Cambridge, Massachusetts: Avalon Publishing Group, Inc., 2006), 186.

17 Kross, Ethan, *The Voice In Our Head, Why It Matters, and How To Harness It* (Crown Trade Paperback Edition, 2022).

18 Burke, Jude Miller, and Attridge, Mark, "Pathways to Career and Leadership Success: Part 1 – A Psychosocial Profile of $100k Professionals," *Journal of Workplace Behavioral Health* 26 (2011):175–206. Phases 1 and 2 of the study were published in this journal. Phases 3 and 4 are currently unpublished. See also, Jude Miller Burke and Mark Attridge, "Pathways to Career and Leadership Success, Part 2: Striking Gender Similarities Among $100k Professionals," *Journal of Workplace Behavioral Health* 26:207–239.

19 Judge, T. A., Erez, A., Bono, J. E., and Thoresen, C. J., "The Core Self-Evaluation Scale Development of a Measure," *Personnel Psychology* 56a, no. 2 (2003): 303–331.

20 Burke, Jude Miller, "Career hurdles: Gender bias and abuse trauma." Presented at the annual convention of the American Psychological Association, Toronto, Ontario, Canada, (August 2015).

21 Burke, Jude Miller, and Attridge, Mark, "Pathways to Career and Leadership Success: Part 1 – A Psychosocial Profile of $100k Professionals," *Journal of Workplace Behavioral Health* 26 (2011): 175–206. Phases 1 and 2 of the study were published in this journal. Phases 3 and 4 are currently unpublished. See also, Jude Miller Burke and Mark Attridge, "Pathways to Career and Leadership Success, Part 2: Striking Gender Similarities Among $100k Professionals," *Journal of Workplace Behavioral Health* 26:207–239.

22 Tawwab, Nedra, *Set Boundaries, Find Peace,: a guide to reclaiming yourself*, Penguin Random House, 2021, p.7

23 Burke, Jude Miller, and Attridge, Mark, "Pathways to Career and Leadership Success: Part 1 – A Psychosocial Profile of $100k Professionals," *Journal of Workplace Behavioral Health* 26 (2011): 175–206. Phases 1 and 2 of the study were published in this journal. Phases 3 and 4 are currently unpublished. See also, Jude Miller Burke and Mark Attridge, "Pathways to Career and Leadership Success, Part 2: Striking Gender Similarities Among $100k Professionals," *Journal of Workplace Behavioral Health*, 26:207–239.

24 Tannen, Deborah, *Talking From 9 to 5: Women and Men at Work* (New York: William Morrow, 2001), 300.

25 Weitzman, Susan, *Not to People Like Us: Hidden Abuse in Upscale Marriages* (New York: Basic Books, 2000), 18.

26 Evans, Patricia, *The Verbally Abusive Relationship: How to Recognize It and How to Respond* (Avon: Massachusetts, 2010), 202.

27 Ibid.

28 Burke, Jude Miller, *The Millionaire Mystique: How Working Women Become Wealthy & You Can, Too!* (Boston & London: Nicholas Brealey, 2014), 237–242.

29 Toplak, M. E., West, R. F., and Stanovich, K. E., "The Cognitive Reflection Test as a Predictor of Performance on Heuristics-and-biases Tasks," *Memory and Cognition* (2011) 39:1275 doi:10.3758/s13421-011-0104-1.

30 Boyce, T. W. & Ellis, B. J. "Biological Sensitivity to Context: An Evolutionary-Developmental Theory of the Origins and Functions of Stress Reactivity," *Development and Psychopathology* 17 (2005): 271–301.

31 McGonigal, Kelly, *The Upside of Stress: Why Stress Is Good For You and How to Get Good At It* (New York: Penguin Random House, 2015), 30.

32 Burke, S., Rodriguez, S., Miller Burke, Jude, *The Impact of the Pandemic on Young Adults: Adaptive Behaviors and Recommendations,* September 2021.

33 Ibid.

34 Southwick, Steven M. and Charney, Dennis S., "Enhance Your Resilience," *Scientific American Mind* 24, no. 3 (July 2013): 32–41.

35 Clear, James, *Atomic Habits: An Easy & Proven Way to Build Good Habits & Break Bad Ones* (Avery-Penguin Random House, 2018), 253.

36 Ibid.

www.ingramcontent.com/pod-product-compliance
Lightning Source LLC
LaVergne TN
LVHW090939080826
845145LV00003B/820

* 9 7 8 1 9 6 2 8 3 4 1 3 1 *